ANGELS ON ASSIGNMENT

7 True Stories of Divine Intervention

Including the Policeman Unable To Arrest Christians in China & the Chicago Firefighter Led Through Flames to Safety

PASTOR JOE LIGHTHALL

ISBN 978-1-918219-06-7

First Edition: 2025
Published by: Cosmic Jive Publishing

www.cosmicjivepublishing.com

For permissions and inquiries, contact:
info@cosmicjivepublishing.com

Follow Pastor Joe

ABOUT THE AUTHOR

Joe Lighthall has served as a pastor in the American Midwest for many years. Before that, he worked as a missionary in Eastern Europe, traveling behind the Iron Curtain during the Cold War. Those years included carrying Bibles across borders where the Scriptures were forbidden, meeting with believers in hidden house churches, and witnessing first-hand how faith endured under persecution.

Since the 1970s, he has listened to, gathered, and carefully preserved stories of encounters with angels—accounts that span continents, cultures, and generations.

His approach has always been both pastoral and discerning. While he treasures the testimonies entrusted to him, he does not take every story at face value. Instead, he prayerfully seeks to verify what he can, weighing each account with Scripture and with common sense. His aim is not to sensationalize, but to offer encouragement to those who wonder whether heaven still breaks into earth.

Over the decades, he has come to see that these stories—whether dramatic or ordinary—carry a common thread: God's people are never truly alone. Angels, as the Bible reminds us, are "ministering spirits sent to serve those who will inherit salvation" (Hebrews 1:14).

The author continues to welcome new accounts from readers. If you or someone you know has experienced a moment you cannot explain—a brush with the divine, a presence that comforted or protected you—he would be honored to hear from you. These stories not only strengthen the faith of those who tell them, but also encourage countless others to believe that God still works in quiet and surprising ways today.

You can contact Joe via his publisher: put 'Pastor Joe' in the subject line and email

info@cosmicjivepublishing.com

Contents

Author's Note on Testimonies & Confidentiality

The stories in this book are true accounts. While many individuals boldly embrace their testimonies and are unashamed to be named, others—such as family members, friends, or those connected to these events—have not given explicit permission to be identified. To respect their privacy, some names, locations and identifying details have been changed. However, the divine encounters and spiritual truths remain unchanged.

Every effort has been made to present these testimonies with accuracy and respect. If any story unintended resembles a reader's personal experience without direct acknowledgment, it is entirely coincidental.

Note to the Reader

You hold in your hands a book of testimonies. They are accounts— reports told by men and women whose lives were interrupted by something they could not explain. Some are simple. Others are harrowing. All are offered with sincerity.

These pages are filled with accounts from very different corners of the world: firehouses in Chicago, secret churches in China, the quiet spaces of hospital rooms and ordinary homes. But the thread running through them is the same. When fear pressed in, heaven pressed closer.

You may read them with skepticism. That is understandable. Angels do not fit neatly into modern categories. For many of us, the world has been explained in terms of science and psychology, sociology and politics. To speak of unseen beings who intervene in the affairs of human lives feels, at best, quaint; at worst, naïve.

I do not ask you to set aside your reason. I only ask you to listen with the same courtesy you would offer to any witness in a courtroom. Testimony deserves hearing, even when it unsettles our assumptions.

Across history, the church has carried such testimonies. From the book of Acts, where chains fell from prisoners and light shone in cells, to the annals of the martyrs, where men and women sang on their way to execution, there has always been a chorus of witness insisting: *we were not alone.* These are not footnotes of piety. They are central to the lived experience of Christians under pressure.

In this second volume of my When Heaven Steps In series, the stories lean especially into that context of pressure. They come not only from everyday brushes with danger, but from the furnace of persecution. They are set in places where faith is costly, where confession of Christ can mean arrest, where gathering for prayer requires secrecy, where courage is tested in the harshest conditions.

I have had the privilege — and the burden — of hearing many such accounts firsthand. In my younger years, I was a missionary behind the Iron Curtain. My time in Eastern Europe taught me something about fear, about risk, and about the extraordinary ways God sustains His people when all human strength runs out.

This book gathers a handful of those accounts. Some come from the persecuted church in Asia. Others from individuals whose lives, though far from persecution, still brushed against the mystery of the unseen. They are varied in setting but united in theme: heaven draws near.

These testimonies are told simply. They are not dramatized for spectacle, though at times they carry drama enough of their own. They are not arguments, though they may provoke questions. They are not meant to be exhaustive, but illustrative. Each one is a window, opening just a little onto a larger reality.

Many believers suffer without visions, without luminous figures, without miraculous interventions. Some die alone, their prayers unanswered in the way they had hoped. These stories do not erase that grief. They do not suggest that faith guarantees deliverance. Rather, they remind us that even in the midst of suffering, God sometimes allows glimpses of His nearness. They are signs, not formulas.

You should remember the testimony of the then unbelieving policeman: he was able to see an angel standing guard for the persecuted church: but the Christians in hiding just yards away from him saw nothing. How many times may there be angels around you unseen but doing their silent work?

If you are reading this as a skeptic, I welcome you. Your questions are fair. Testimony can be tested, weighed, examined. But I ask you not to dismiss too quickly. Consider at least this possibility: if even one of these accounts is true, then the world is larger, more porous, more mysterious than we imagine.

And if you are reading this as a believer, I hope you find encouragement. They are reminders that you are part of a story far greater than your own, a story in which God's care for His people has never wavered.

I do not ask you to suspend reason. I ask only that you leave room for mystery. So turn the page, and read with me. Not for spectacle. Not for certainty. But for wonder.

Because sometimes, when the night is darkest and the danger most severe, Heaven Steps In.

Introduction
When the Unseen Draws Near

There are nights when the air itself feels fragile. Nights when fear presses so close that breath becomes shallow and time stumbles forward in hesitant steps. A house engulfed in flame. A knock at the door when the communist authorities come for house church worshippers. A diagnosis that drops like a blade. These are the moments when human strength falters, when no training or wit or wealth can guarantee survival. In such moments, our natural senses tell us the story is over—that there is no way through.

And yet, sometimes, just as the world seems to collapse, something—or Someone—steps near. Again and again, I have heard stories of something else breaking in. Not the absence of danger, but the arrival of presence. Not escape from suffering, but a companion in the midst of it. Something unseen. Someone unseen.

More and often than not, it is not with spectacle, a fanfare of trumpets or cinematic rescues. But with a presence. A shift in the atmosphere. A supernatural calm that makes no sense given the chaos. A glimpse, however fleeting, of the unseen.

I have listened to a firefighter tell me how a figure guided him through a blazing building when all exits were sealed. The boy he rescued who whispered, "I saw him too." I have sat in a small apartment in Asia, hearing believers whisper of light in a prison cell that no guard could extinguish. I have read accounts from men and women whose rational minds wrestled with what their eyes had seen, unable to fit it into the neat categories of psychology or propaganda.

And I have carried my own memories. In the days when I crossed borders with forbidden books hidden in vehicle compartments, I knew the taste of fear. I knew the pounding heart when guards pawed through luggage, the silent prayers whispered under my breath. More than once, I felt the atmosphere shift — a guard distracted, a barrier inexplicably removed, a way made where none should have been. I do not claim visions or voices at the time, only this: I knew I was not alone.

These testimonies, mine and others, share a common thread: they are not arguments. They are not neat proofs to be wielded in debate. They are witness. And witness is stubborn. It does not bow easily to explanation.

The skeptic has ready answers. Adrenaline. Hallucination. Collective suggestion. I do not dismiss these too quickly. The human mind is fragile under pressure; the body does strange things in extremity. And yet, time after time, I have listened to stories where explanation is thinner than the testimony it seeks to contain. A police officer who mocked faith, later confessing that an angelic presence literally barred him from his duty. A seamstress who emerged from prison more radiant than when she entered, not because the beatings were gentle but because the cell was filled with light.

These - when spoken - are not tales polished for spectacle. They are recounted haltingly, sometimes with tears, sometimes with the embarrassed laughter of people who know how unbelievable they sound. They are not offered to win arguments. They are offered because the truth of them burned too deep to stay unspoken.

The first book in this series gathered a handful of such accounts — men and women whose lives were pierced by heaven's nearness in ways they never expected. Their stories stood like cairns on a mountain path, markers pointing toward the reality that the unseen sometimes steps into the seen.

This second book continues that journey, but it does not repeat it. The testimonies here are different — darker, in some ways. They are set not only in the quiet corners of daily life, but in the crucible of danger and persecution. Fires that should have consumed. Prisons that should have crushed. Governments that tried to silence. These are stories drawn from the edge of survival, where heaven's presence is not a luxury but a lifeline.

I have been struck, in listening to them, by the pattern that emerges: heaven's messengers appear both to the faithful and to the faithless. To the believer in chains, offering courage. To the skeptic with authority, offering rebuke. Sometimes to rescue, sometimes to confront, always to remind: the church is not abandoned, and the world is more porous than we dare to admit.

This is not new. The history of the church is studded with such accounts. The book of Acts tells of Peter, bound between guards, his wrists heavy with chains, when suddenly a light filled the cell and an angel struck his side, waking him to freedom. Centuries later, in the Roman arenas, martyrs went to their deaths singing, some describing visions of radiant figures who met them in the dust before the lions. In every generation where faith has been pressed hard, stories of the unseen breaking through have risen.

During the Reformation, believers smuggling forbidden Scripture into hostile lands wrote of close escapes they could not explain, of watchmen inexplicably turning their heads. In the Soviet gulags, brothers and sisters testified to voices in the night urging them to sing, and to a strength that baffled their captors. In our own time, the underground churches of China, Iran, and North Korea quietly tell stories of doors that will not yield, of guards who falter, of light that fills cells where darkness should reign.

Always the same thread: God has not abandoned His people.

When I smuggled Bibles across the Iron Curtain, I met this reality often, though in quieter ways. Once, at a checkpoint between Germany and what is now the Czech republic, a guard barked at me to open the boot of my car. Inside were hundreds of New Testaments, carefully hidden but by no means invisible to those who knew what they were looking for. I remember the taste of fear, metallic in my mouth. I remember praying, *Lord, if You do not intervene, all is lost.*

The guard began to search — and then, inexplicably, he stopped. His eyes glazed as though distracted by something behind me. He slammed the boot shut and waved me through. To this day I cannot explain it. I only know the relief that poured through me and the certainty that I was not alone.

Another time, while hiding items under blankets in a van, I felt an inexplicable calm descend. Not bravado, not denial of risk, but a steadying presence. Later I learned that at that very hour, believers in another country were praying for me. Presence and intercession braided together.

And yet another time again, we were led to dump our cargo in a river, hoping the packages would float to believers downstream just before our vehicle was unexpectedly intercepted. (They did - against the odds).

And then another time again, where I was literally beaten for my faith. Stop talking, I was told. I refused and in that moment, as several men tore at my limbs, I felt the divine peace that passes all understanding - knowing I was not alone.

It is from that posture — one who has brushed the edge of the unseen — that I receive these newer stories. I gather them as echoes of a pattern I recognize. The one common thread is they point to a Presence with believers. And a Presence calling to non believers to come home.

Why angels? Why not always the voice of God directly, or the sudden miracle of release? Scripture hints at the answer. Angels are servants, messengers, embodiments of God's care in tangible form. They lead Peter past sleeping guards. They minister to Jesus in the wilderness. They are not meant to eclipse God Himself, but to embody His nearness in moments when flesh-and-blood fear threatens to overwhelm flesh-and-blood faith.

So too in these testimonies. The angel is not the center; God is. But the angel is the reminder, in blazing clarity, that God has not forgotten.

Skeptics will always ask: "But why them? Why a firefighter in Chicago and not the dozens who perish in other fires? Why Mei in her cell and not the countless others who died unseen and uncomforted?" These are not trivial questions. They pierce at the mystery of suffering, the unevenness of miracles.

I do not pretend to have final answers. I only know

that when heaven steps in, it is never random. It is always purposeful — to strengthen, to confront, to remind. The mystery does not lessen the testimony; it deepens it.

Perhaps, then, these stories are not given to explain suffering but to remind us that suffering is not abandonment. That is the heartbeat of this book. Not triumphalism. Not spectacle. Simply this: we are not left alone.

If you have ever felt the shadow of fear in your own life — not in prison cells or border crossings, perhaps, but in hospital corridors, or sleepless nights of anxiety, or losses that pressed the air from your lungs — then these stories are for you. They are not foreign curiosities, but witnesses to a reality that touches us all. For if God is near to them, He is near to us.

So I invite you: read on. Enter these testimonies not as proofs but as witnesses. Hear them with the ears of wonder. Hold them with reverence. Let them challenge your cynicism and stir your faith. And perhaps, as you turn these pages, you may find yourself whispering, as so many before you have:

I was not alone.

Testimony 1
The Firefighter in the Flames

Some people inherit quiet professions — the steady accounting of numbers, the measured rhythm of teaching, the orderly flow of office life. Jose García had inherited fire.

Fire is both beautiful and merciless. It dances in colors that mesmerize the eye, yet it devours with a hunger that never stops. To a firefighter, it is both enemy and calling —a force to be battled again and again, even at great cost.

Captain Jose García had fought fires for nearly twenty years in Chicago. He had pulled children from burning bedrooms, battled warehouse infernos, and watched homes collapse in showers of sparks. He knew the language of flames, the roar that meant a flashover was coming, the hiss that meant a roof was weakening. He trusted his training, his instincts, and the brothers and sisters in his unit. He learned that bravery was not the absence of fear but the decision to step forward anyway.

But one night, during a blaze that should have ended his life, Jose García discovered something his training could never explain.

The call came just after midnight. A three-story apartment building in the heart of the city was engulfed. Families had fled into the street, some barefoot, others clutching pets, all of them shouting the same thing: someone was still inside. Jose exchanged a glance with his lieutenant — a silent acknowledgment of the stakes.

Jose and his crew rushed in. Smoke clawed at their lungs, flames chewed through stairwells, the building groaned under its own weight. The radio crackled with frantic updates.

"Second floor clear!"

"Fire spreading to the third!"

"Possible victim in unit 3B!"

Jose took the lead, his heart pounding beneath his gear. He had run into burning buildings a hundred times before, but this one felt different—more unstable, more dangerous.

Still, a child might be trapped. And that left no choice.

They reached the third floor, visibility near zero. Heat pressed against them like a furnace. The structure groaned with each shift — a warning that time was measured in seconds, not minutes. Jose barked orders to his crew, then forced his way into unit 3B.

The flames had already gutted the living room. Furniture smoldered, ceiling beams crackled.

Jose pushed through the smoke, scanning every corner.

Then he heard it—a faint cough.

"Hello?" he shouted, his voice muffled by the mask.

Another cough, this time from the bedroom.

Jose plunged forward. There, huddled against the wall, was a little boy, maybe six years old, eyes wide with terror. His small hands clutched a stuffed bear singed by the flames.

"I've got you!" Jose cried, scooping him up.

The boy clung to his neck, coughing violently. Jose turned back toward the hallway—just as the ceiling groaned and collapsed in a shower of sparks, cutting off their exit.

For a moment, Jose froze. Fire surged where the doorway had been, an impassable wall of flame. The heat was unbearable, the air unbreathable. The boy whimpered in his arms, burying his face against his shoulder.

Jose's training told him to look for a secondary exit. But the windows were barred. The fire was spreading too fast. His crew was on the other side of the flames, shouting into their radios, but no path remained.

Trapped.

The boy whimpered, burying his face against Jose's shoulder. Jose's chest tightened, not from smoke alone but from the weight of impending doom. He thought of his wife Neus. He thought of his children. He thought of all the families he had comforted after a loss, and the bitter taste of being on the other side of that grief.

Jose's chest tightened. He whispered the kind of prayer firefighters rarely admit: "God, help us."

The prayer was barely audible beneath the roar of the fire. Just three words, swallowed almost as soon as they left his lips.

Jose hadn't planned to pray. In twenty years of firefighting, he had whispered plenty of quick petitions before climbing ladders or breaking into smoke-filled apartments. But this was different. This was the raw plea of a man who had no other plan.

And then—it happened.

The roar of the fire dulled, as though someone had turned down the volume. Jose felt a sudden calm, so stark it startled him. In the haze of smoke, a figure appeared—tall, luminous, steady. It stood between him and the wall of flame, as if shielding him.

Jose blinked, wondering if the deprivation of oxygen had finally broken his grip on reality. But the figure did not dissolve. It grew clearer.

The figure lifted an arm, and for reasons Jose could never explain, the fire seemed to recoil. The heat eased. The flames bent, as though pressed back by an invisible wind.

"Go," a voice said—not through the ears but inside the heart.

Jose blinked in disbelief, but his feet moved. He stumbled forward, clutching the boy, stepping through where the fire had just raged. Somehow, impossibly, the flames parted enough for him to pass.

Cradling the boy, he stepped forward into the breach. Where seconds earlier an impassable wall of fire had raged, there was now a narrow corridor. The air cooled enough to breathe, the heat lifted enough to run.

He stumbled through, boots pounding over debris, his arms tightening around the child. The figure did not follow, or perhaps it simply remained beyond the veil of smoke. Jose dared one glance back and caught only the impression of radiance dissolving into haze.

A moment later, he burst into the hallway, coughing, but alive. His crew rushed toward him, eyes wide.

"How did you—? We thought you were gone!"

Jose couldn't answer. He only held the boy tighter, whispering through the mask, "We're safe. We're safe."

The crowd erupted in cries and gasps. A woman screamed, clutching her son as Jose handed him into her arms. Neighbors swarmed, firefighters shouted updates, EMTs pressed oxygen masks over faces. Jose staggered to the curb and collapsed onto the back of the engine, yanking off his own mask, chest heaving.

He was alive. The boy was alive.

The fire was finally contained just before dawn. Ash drifted through the air like gray snow, the building reduced to a blackened skeleton. Residents huddled in blankets on the curb, watching as firefighters rolled up hoses and packed gear.

Jose sat on the back of the engine, helmet in his hands, the boy safe now in the care of paramedics. His body trembled from exhaustion, but it wasn't just fatigue. It was something deeper—a disorientation he couldn't shake.

He kept replaying the moment in the bedroom: the roar of the flames, the collapse of the ceiling, the hopelessness—and then the figure. The radiance. The calm. The impossible path through fire.

He could not shake the memory of that figure, the peace that had steadied his steps when there should have been none.

He shook his head hard, muttering to himself, "No one's going to believe this." He was not sure he believed it himself. Except he knew in a place beyond belief that it had happened.

At the debrief, his crew peppered him with questions.

"How did you get through?"

"That fire was a wall—you shouldn't have made it out."

"Seriously, Cap, what happened in there?"

Jose hesitated. He could tell them about the figure. He could tell them about the voice, the fire that bent like reeds in the wind. But would they laugh? Write him off as delirious?

In the end, he said simply, "I don't know. I just… found a way."

The others exchanged doubtful looks but didn't press. Firefighting was full of close calls. Sometimes survival defied explanation. Still, Jose saw it in their eyes: they knew this had been more than luck.

That night, when he finally returned home, Jose sat in the quiet of his living room. His wife, Neus, brought him tea and sat across from him.

"What's wrong?"

He hesitated, then told her everything. About the figure. The radiance. The fire that retreated. The voice that spoke inside him.

Neus listened without interruption. When he finished, she reached across the table and took his hand. "Don't you be doubting what you saw."

Jose swallowed hard. "It felt real. More real than anything. But it seems so crazy that even though I know it happened, part of me wonders if I imagined it."

She squeezed his hand and stated the obvious. "Imaginations don't part flames."

Still, Jose wrestled. Days passed, and the image haunted him. In the firehouse, surrounded by banter and routine, he kept silent. In his own heart, though, the memory burned.

And then came the boy.

Two days later, his family visited the firehouse. They brought cookies, still warm in foil pans, as a gesture of gratitude. The boy, dressed in a superhero T-shirt, ran to Jose.

"You're my hero," the boy whispered.

Jose crouched down, eye to eye. "No, buddy. I just did my job."

The boy blinked, looked around the firehouse expectantly. "Where's the shiny man?"

Jose froze. "You… what?"

The boy nodded. "The shiny man. The one who told me not to be scared." The boy looked around, fully expecting to see him in the station. "Where is he?"

For a moment, Jose could only stare, his throat tight,

his eyes stinging. Whatever doubts had lingered were swept away by the simple, matter-of-fact testimony of a child.

He had not imagined it. They had not been alone. The memory was too clear. The peace too real. And now the boy's words echoed louder than his last grains of 'rational' logic.

Jose kept the boy's words close, like an ember glowing in his chest. *The shiny man. He told me not to be scared.* Those words did not fit neatly into the report he submitted to headquarters. They lived elsewhere—in the quiet space between fear and wonder.

He didn't share them widely at first. Some things are too sacred to throw carelessly into the noise of skepticism. But slowly, in quiet conversations, he let the story slip.

The first time was with his lieutenant, Ramirez, a grizzled firefighter who had seen more than his share of tragedy. They sat together in the truck bay one evening, sipping bitter coffee, watching the engines gleam under fluorescent lights.

"You've been different since that fire," Ramirez said bluntly. "Calmer. Like you're carrying something."

Ramirez was not a man given to superstition. But something in his tone made honesty feel possible.

Jose hesitated. "Maybe I am."

So he told him. About the voice, the figure, the flames that bent. And finally, about the boy confirming it.

Ramirez leaned back, his brow furrowed. For a long time he said nothing. Then he murmured, "My abuela used to say angels walk with us in fire. I never believed her. Maybe I should have."

The two men sat in silence, the weight of memory and mystery pressing in. Neither man said more. They simply sipped coffee in silence, the weight of memory pressing close.

Word spread, not as gossip but as testimony. Some firefighters rolled their eyes. "García's getting mystical," they joked. But others leaned closer, asking him to repeat it, whispering their own near-misses, their own moments they couldn't explain.

One younger recruit confessed, "Cap, there was a time I thought I saw someone in a smoke-filled hallway, pointing me toward the exit. I thought I was losing it. Hearing your story… maybe I wasn't."

García realized then that he wasn't alone—not only in the fire, but in the hidden stories firefighters carried and rarely voiced. Stories of protection, of whispers in chaos, of unseen hands pulling them back from death.

These stories had always existed, circulating quietly in the background, dismissed as tricks of the mind. But Jose's testimony, coupled with the child's confirmation, gave them new weight. They were no longer oddities; they were part of a pattern.

At home, Jose found his faith quietly rekindling. He and Neus began attending church again, slipping into the back pews. He didn't make a show of it. He didn't stand to speak. But he listened with a new attentiveness, as if every hymn and sermon resonated with the echo of that voice in the flames.

At home, Neus noticed the change as well. He prayed more often, quietly, before meals or before sleep. He opened his Bible with a seriousness she had not seen in years. He carried himself differently—not invincible, but steady, as though the fire had burned away more than wood and plaster.

One Sunday, the pastor preached from Daniel 3—the story of Shadrach, Meshach, and Abednego in the fiery furnace. Jose felt his breath catch as he heard the words aloud: *"And the fourth man looked like a son of the gods."*

He gripped Neus's hand. The story wasn't ancient anymore. It was his.

Eventually, the local news caught wind of the rescue. Cameras came to the station, praising Jose as a hero. He gave the interviews politely but refused to claim the spotlight.

"I didn't do it alone," he said firmly.

The reporters assumed he meant his crew. Jose didn't correct them. Some truths, he knew, were better shared heart to heart than on television.

But for those who asked, those who really wanted to know, he told the fuller version. Always with humility. Always with gratitude.

In time, the story reached beyond the firehouse. A local pastor invited him to speak at a men's breakfast. Jose resisted at first — he was not a preacher, and the idea of telling his story in public unsettled him. But Neus encouraged him gently. "It's not about making speeches," she said. "It's about giving thanks."

So he told it. Slowly. Carefully. Without drama. Just the facts of what he saw, what the boy confirmed, and what lingered after. The men in the room leaned forward, the clink of forks forgotten. When he finished, silence hung heavy. Then one man, eyes wet, said simply, "I needed to hear that."

Jose realized then that the story was not his to hoard. It was a gift to steward. He spoke of what he saw but told also of the inexplicable sense of peace in those moments. The inexplicable calm that wrapped him in the moment of greatest terror. The sense that the universe itself leaned near and whispered: *You are not alone.*

The story never stopped shaping Jose. It didn't make him reckless, assuming every fire would part before him. He still respected the danger, still trained hard, still wept for those lost. But it gave him a steadiness, a conviction that he was never truly alone in the flames.

Reflection — The God Who Walks in Fire

Fire is unforgiving. It consumes without hesitation, devours without remorse, leaves only ash in its wake. To step into it willingly, as firefighters do, is an act of courage few can fathom. And yet, even there, in the hottest crucibles of human fear, the testimonies continue to emerge: *we were not alone.*

Jose's story is not unique in its shape, though it is remarkable in its clarity. A wall of flames that should have taken him and the boy. A figure of light, radiant and steady. A voice that spoke not to the ears but to the soul: *Go.* A way made where no way existed.

It echoes the ancient furnace of Babylon, where three faithful men stood unconsumed and a fourth man walked beside them. It resonates with Isaiah's promise: *"When you walk through the fire, you will not be burned; the flames will not set you ablaze."* And it humbles us with the reminder that these are not just poetic metaphors but lived realities for some, even in our own time.

Skeptics will, of course, dismiss it. Heat, smoke, adrenaline—they can all play tricks on perception. And yet, dismissals falter before the testimony of both Jose and the boy. Two witnesses, seeing the same figure, remembering the same peace. Two lives shaped not only by survival but by the certainty that mercy intervened. But psychology cannot account for fire that parts.

What makes Jose García's story so striking is he was no romantic novice swept away by adrenaline. He was a veteran captain, trained to keep his head when others lost theirs, hardened by years of routine and loss. When he says he saw something in the smoke, he does not mean it lightly.

Skeptics have quick responses. They speak of hypoxia, hallucination, adrenaline-induced visions. And these must be acknowledged. We live in a world where the human brain is fragile under stress. It would be naïve to dismiss natural explanations out of hand.

But what do we do with the boy? A child too young to know the scripts of religious vision, who described the "shiny man" in words Jose himself had not supplied. A child who, in the innocent bluntness of youth, confirmed that he too had been calmed by presence. Coincidence? Collective delusion? Or testimony that resists easy dismissal?

The Bible does not shy away from fire. It names it as both judgment and purification, danger and glory. Isaiah does not promise God's people that they will avoid flames; he promises that when they walk through them, they will not be consumed. Daniel's friends do not escape the furnace; they meet a fourth figure inside it. Fire is not removed, but Presence transforms it.

Jose's testimony falls into that same lineage. He did not avoid the blaze. He entered it, as he had entered countless others. But there, when his strength and training were exhausted, the unseen drew near. The figure did not preach, did not explain, did not dazzle. It simply made a way where there was none. That is the shape of biblical deliverance: not spectacle, but salvation; not absence of trial, but presence within it.

The temptation in hearing such stories is to treat them

as formulas. We imagine that if we pray the right words or muster the right faith, angels will appear on demand. But testimonies resist such domestication. Jose himself admitted he did not know why God intervened in that moment and not in others. He had attended funerals of comrades. He had wept with families who received no miracle. And still, the fact remained: one night, in one furnace, heaven stooped near.

That tension is the crucible of faith. We want certainty; God often gives mystery. We want guarantees; God offers presence. We want deliverance from every fire; God promises only that we will not face them alone.

What, then, is the use of Jose's story? It is not a manual for avoiding loss. It is not proof against the skeptic or ammunition for argument. It is, rather, a witness. A signpost. A reminder that the world is more porous than we imagine, that the boundary between seen and unseen is thinner than smoke.

For some, that reminder will stir hope. For others, it will stir unease. That is as it should be. Encounters with the holy rarely leave us neutral. They unsettle, they invite, they provoke questions we might rather avoid.

But consider this: if even once in human history, flames bent back at the command of an unseen messenger; if even once a firefighter and a child glimpsed a figure who calmed their terror — then perhaps the world is charged with more mercy than we dare believe. Perhaps presence is closer than absence. Perhaps the peace Jose described is not anomaly but invitation.

And for those who walk through their own fires — the fires of diagnosis, betrayal, loss, fear — Jose's story whispers a quiet encouragement. Not that flames will vanish, but that you may find a strange calm in the center of them. Not that you will be spared all grief, but that you may one day look back and say with trembling conviction: *I was not alone.*

Testimony 2
The Visitors at the Bedside

Children should not die before their parents. That is the order we cling to, the rule that makes life feel bearable. Parents age, parents fade, parents go first—that is how the story is supposed to go. When the script is broken, when the small coffin must be carried instead of the large, the world itself feels like it has betrayed its own laws.

The Washingtons knew that betrayal all too well.

Their son, Caleb, had been a whirlwind of life: a boy with mud on his shoes, grass in his hair, and questions that tumbled out faster than his parents could answer them. He loved baseball, pancakes drowned in syrup, and stories about knights who never lost their way.

Then came the diagnosis. Leukemia. A word that fell into their lives like a stone through glass. The doctors spoke of treatment plans, percentages, protocols. The family clung to hope as months of hospital visits, needles, and transfusions blurred together. Caleb endured it with a bravery that shamed even the adults around him, smiling through the nausea, cracking jokes with the nurses, asking when he could go home to his dog.

But the treatments failed.

By the time winter came, the doctors spoke more softly. Words like *comfort care* replaced words like *cure.*

The Washingtons knew, though they could not bear to say it aloud: their son was dying.

The hospice room was painted in cheerful colors, a feeble attempt to mask its true purpose. A quilt from home lay over Caleb's small body. His parents sat beside him, one on each side, holding hands across his narrow frame as if they could form a shield against what was coming.

Caleb drifted in and out of sleep, his body frail, his voice weak. But one afternoon, as snow fell outside the window, he stirred suddenly, his eyes bright, more alert than they had been in weeks.

"Mom," he whispered. "Do you see them?"

His mother leaned closer. "See who, sweetheart?"

"The people," Caleb said, his gaze fixed on a corner of the room. "They're shiny. Like… like light. They're smiling."

His father glanced at his mother, heart twisting. She forced a smile. "Maybe you're dreaming."

But Caleb shook his head, insistent. "No. They're real. They're right there." His eyes shining "They say I don't have to be scared no more."

The Washingtons exchanged helpless looks. They wanted to believe him. Their rational thinking told them to dismiss it as morphine, fever, imagination. But Caleb's face glowed with a serenity they hadn't seen in months.

"They say they'll take me to the garden," he whispered, eyes never leaving the unseen visitors. "It's beautiful there. So many colors. You'll like it when you come."

Tears spilled down his mother's cheeks. She stroked his hair, unable to speak. His father turned away, shoulders shaking.

Caleb looked back at them, his voice suddenly steady. "Don't cry. Death is not the end. It's only the beginning. You'll see."

The vision came again in the days that followed. Sometimes Caleb would speak of the garden, sometimes of a river with bridges made of light, sometimes of a great house filled with music. Always, the radiant visitors were there—watching, waiting, comforting.

"They're not in a hurry," he explained once, as though he understood more than he should. "They'll stay until I'm ready."

The nurses, used to such stories, nodded gently when his parents told them. "Children see things," one said softly. "Near the end, it's not unusual." But even she admitted that the peace on Caleb's face was remarkable.

For the Washingtons, the visions became both comfort and torment. Comfort, because their boy was no longer afraid. Torment, because every description was a reminder of how close he was to leaving them.

One evening, as the sun bled orange over the snow, Caleb called them both close.

"They're telling me it's soon," he whispered. "But it's okay. I'll go with them."

His mother clutched his hand. "We love you, Caleb. More than anything."

"Goodbye isn't forever" he said, smiling faintly. "And when you come, you'll see the garden."

That night, Caleb slipped quietly away.

His parents, Dwayne and Precious, were shattered. And yet, beneath their grief, they carried the strange, steady knowledge that their son had not gone alone.

* * *

The house was unbearable without him.

After the funeral, after the casseroles stopped arriving and the neighbors stopped checking in, silence swallowed the Washington home. His baseball glove still hung by the back door. His shoes still sat, muddy, in the hallway. His laughter—once ricocheting off every wall—was replaced by an emptiness so vast it seemed to echo.

His parents moved through the days like shadows. They spoke little. Meals went untouched. Nights stretched into hours of tears muffled into pillows. The only thing they shared was the ache.

But beneath the grief lay something stranger, more complicated: the memory of Caleb's words.

"They're shiny. Like light. They say I don't have to be scared."

"They'll stay until I'm ready."

"I'll show you the garden."

The images clung to them, bright and terrible.

Precious wanted to believe. She replayed his descriptions, clutched at them like lifelines. She imagined her boy running through a radiant garden, free of pain, laughing again. At night, she whispered into the darkness, "Show him to me. Just once more. Please."

Dwayne, however, resisted. A practical man, he could not reconcile what Caleb had said with what he believed to be true. Morphine dreams, he told himself. The brain's way of soothing a dying child. Better to cling to science than to fairy tales.

But his son's words haunted him all the same.

One night, after Precious had fallen asleep, Dwayne sat alone in Caleb's room. He ran his hands over the quilt folded at the end of the bed, breathing in the faint scent of his boy's shampoo. He stared at the empty space where his son should have been.

"If it wasn't real," he whispered, voice breaking, "why did he look so at peace?"

The tension between them grew. Precious needed to believe. Dwayne needed to doubt. They argued in hushed tones, neither wanting to dishonor their son, both aching in different ways.

"You think he was just hallucinating?" Precious asked one night, her voice trembling with anger.

"I think his brain was protecting him," Dwayne replied, though his voice lacked conviction. "Is that so terrible? At least he wasn't afraid."

Precious shook her head, tears streaming. "He wasn't afraid because he *saw* something, Dwayne. He *knew* something we don't. Why can't you let yourself believe it?"

Dwayne had no answer.

Their pastor visited, sitting quietly in the living room with them. He listened as Precious poured out her faith and Dwayne his doubts. Finally, he said, "Children have a clarity at the threshold of death that we adults lose. Maybe Caleb was given a gift you weren't meant to see, only to hear. Maybe your job now is to hold that gift, even if you don't understand it."

Precious clung to those words. Dwayne, though unconvinced, couldn't shake them either.

In the weeks that followed, strange things began to happen.

One afternoon, Precious found a feather—perfectly white, gleaming—resting on Caleb's windowsill, though the window had been shut tight. Another time, as Dwayne drove home from work, a song came on the radio—the very hymn sung at Caleb's funeral. He nearly pulled over, the ache so sharp it felt like a blade.

Coincidences, perhaps. But they unsettled Dwayne, nudged at the edges of his disbelief.

And at night, he dreamed of Caleb. Not the frail boy in the hospice bed, but strong, laughing, running through fields he didn't recognize. In the dream, Caleb always turned to him and said, "I'm okay, Dad. I'm not alone."

Dwayne woke each time with tears on his face.

The Washingtons carried on. Grief didn't leave—it simply reshaped itself, settling into their bones. They went back to work, back to routines, back to a life that looked the same from the outside but was forever altered inside.

But even in their different ways of grieving—Precious with faith, Dwayne with doubt—they found themselves drawn again and again to the same words.

"I'll show you the garden."

Neither of them could forget. Neither of them wanted to.

Time, people said, would soften the grief. The Washingtons discovered that wasn't quite true. Time didn't erase their loss; it simply wove it into the fabric of who they were.

Precious began returning to church first. At first, she slipped in quietly, sitting in the back pew where no one could see her cry. The hymns broke her open, reminding her of the hospice room, of Caleb whispering about music in the great house of light. Slowly, though, those same songs began to feel less like knives and more like balm.

She joined a grief support group at the church. When it was her turn to share, she told Caleb's story—not with drama, but with trembling reverence. "He said they came for him," she whispered. "He said he wasn't alone."

Some of the other parents wept. Some nodded. One mother reached for her hand and said, "My daughter heard beautiful music." For the first time, Precious felt less like a woman drowning in sorrow and more like part of a hidden community of the broken who had glimpsed something beyond.

Dwayne's healing came slower. He returned to work, burying himself in long hours and late nights. He kept his doubt like armor, convinced it would protect him from the rawness of hope. But cracks appeared.

One afternoon, a colleague stopped him in the hallway. "I'm sorry about your boy," she said softly. "When my brother was dying, he said he saw the same thing. Bright people, waiting for him. I never forgot it."

Her words unsettled him. Were all these people deluded—or was he the one refusing to see?

That night, Dwayne sat in Caleb's room again, staring at the baseball glove still hanging by the door. He whispered, "If it was real, son, if you really saw them—help me believe."

No answer came. But the room felt less empty.

Months later, Precious convinced him to attend a service. He sat stiffly in the pew, eyes fixed on the stained glass, until the scripture reading began. It was from John's Gospel: *In my Father's house are many rooms. I go to prepare a place for you.*

The words struck him like a hammer. Many rooms. A great house. Music. Caleb's vision surged back with startling clarity. He gripped the pew in front of him, his knuckles white.

Afterward, he said little. But for the first time, he did not push the possibility away.

As seasons turned, the Washingtons found a fragile rhythm of living with absence. Birthdays were hardest. They lit a candle for Caleb, setting it on the table beside his empty chair. Christmas brought both tears and laughter as they hung his favorite ornaments on the tree.

They began volunteering at the children's hospital. Precious read stories to the young patients. Dwayne fixed broken toys, mended wheelchairs, did the quiet work of a man who knew the stakes. More than once, parents in the ward asked how they could endure being there. Precious would squeeze Dwayne's hand and say gently, "Because our son wasn't afraid. He showed us there's more than this."

Their story spread, quietly at first—among church friends, support groups, neighbors. Some dismissed it. Others clung to it. And still others, grieving their own losses, came to them with whispered confessions: "My mother saw them too. My child spoke of gardens too. My husband said he wasn't alone."

The Washingtons never claimed certainty. They didn't need to. They simply carried Caleb's testimony into every space they entered, a light shining softly through their shattered hearts.

"He was very sick," they'd said softly. "But when it was time for him to go, he saw beautiful visitors—bright as light. They told him not to be afraid. And he wasn't."

Reflection — When Children Lead Us

Skeptics will always have their answer. Morphine hallucinations. Oxygen deprivation. The brain, kind enough in its final hours, painting a comforting scene for a child too young to understand what was happening. Science offers these explanations with tidy confidence, and perhaps they are enough for some.

But for those who were there—for parents who watched fear melt from their child's face, for nurses who saw a dying boy speak of gardens and radiant visitors—the explanation feels too thin. The fruit of Caleb's vision was not delirium but peace. And peace is not a symptom to be dismissed.

It is striking how often children, standing at the threshold of death, describe the same things. A glow. Visitors radiant with light. A place of beauty and welcome. Words not borrowed from sermons or theology textbooks, but spoken with the directness of innocence. Adults tend to doubt. Children simply see.

Maybe that is why their testimony carries such weight. They are not angling for belief, not crafting arguments. They are reporting. As Caleb said with quiet certainty: "They'll stay until I'm ready."

What do we do with such testimony?

For the Washingtons, it became both wound and balm. They would always ache for their son. Nothing could make the empty chair at the table disappear. But the visions offered a framework for hope, a reminder that Caleb's story did not end with the hospice room. His last words reframed his death—not as abandonment, but as arrival.

That is not a small gift.

Because if there is one thing grief screams at us, it is the fear of aloneness. That our loved one was swallowed by silence. That their final moment was one of terror. Caleb's story cut through that fear like a shaft of light: *Don't cry. I'm not alone.*

Maybe that is the heart of the message. Not proof of angels, not diagrams of heaven, but the simple assurance that no one crosses alone.

It is a message we need not only in death but in life. For who among us has not felt buried, cornered, afraid? Who among us has not longed for a presence to whisper: *Don't be afraid. You are not alone.*

Children seem to glimpse this more easily. Perhaps because their hearts are uncluttered, their imaginations unashamed, their trust unbroken by years of doubt. Caleb's vision does not scold the skeptic or demand belief. It simply invites us to wonder whether the world is larger, more layered, more merciful than we have dared to think.

The Washingtons have carried that invitation since. For Precious, it has bloomed into faith renewed, the kind that sings through tears. For Dwayne, it became a humbler openness, a loosening of his grip on the need for certainty. Together, they lived with grief and hope intertwined, because their son had shown them what they themselves could not see.

And maybe that is the quiet miracle of such visions: they give courage to the living as much as peace to the dying.

In the end, Caleb's story is not about angels or gardens so much as it is about presence. About the astonishing possibility that when we—or those we love—step into the unknown, we are met, not abandoned.

That is what a little boy, with mud still in his shoes and questions still on his lips, wanted his parents to know. And perhaps, what he wants us to know too.

Testimony 3
Wings in the Storm

Captain Edward "Eddie" Lawson had flown through storms before. In his twenty years as a commercial pilot, he had battled crosswinds that slammed against the fuselage, lightning that lit up the cockpit like a camera flash, turbulence so violent it felt like the plane was being shaken by an angry god. Flying was risk, and risk was his profession.

But nothing compared to that night.

It was late autumn, the kind of evening when the weather reports contradicted one another. His crew had checked the radar: a line of storms moving fast, but breakable, navigable. He'd flown worse. The flight was a short hop from Dallas to Kansas City—two hours, give or take. The passengers boarded, weary business travelers and families bound for home. The doors shut. The engines roared.

At first, all was routine. Climb, level, the steady thrum of turbines. But an hour in, the first jolt hit. Then another. Soon the plane was shuddering as though caught in a giant's fist. Rain hammered the windows. Wind screamed against the metal skin.

"Seatbelt sign on," Eddie told his first officer, voice steady though his pulse raced.

He radioed air traffic control. Static answered. The

storm had swallowed their signal.

Lightning slashed the sky, so bright it seared his vision. The altimeter jumped erratically. The plane pitched, dropped a hundred feet in an instant, then another hundred. Passengers screamed in the cabin.

Eddie gripped the controls, muscles taut. He had been trained for turbulence, but this was more than turbulence. The instruments spun, the plane rolled, his every correction answered by another violent shove from the storm.

"Come on," he muttered through clenched teeth. "Hold together."

But the plane wasn't holding. It was losing.

Later, Eddie would describe the moment in words he never thought he'd use: surrender. He had fought the storm with every ounce of training, every practiced move. But nothing worked. The plane was falling, spiraling, drawn down into blackness.

And then, something impossible happened.

A pressure against his hands. Not his own muscles, not the resistance of the yoke. Something else.

The controls steadied. The wild spin slowed. The nose lifted, smooth and sure, as though guided by invisible strength.

Eddie froze. He was still holding the yoke, but it no longer felt like his grip alone. It was as if another pair of hands had closed over his, stronger, steadier, carrying the weight of the plane with unshakable calm.

The storm still raged, lightning still split the sky—but the panic broke. A peace settled over him, sharp and undeniable.

For the next ten minutes, Eddie flew—or rather, was flown. The pressure on the controls remained, the presence steady, until the clouds finally thinned, the wind eased, and the night sky opened like a curtain.

The plane leveled out. Silence fell in the cockpit, broken only by the ragged sound of his own breathing.

When he glanced at his first officer, the younger man's face was pale, his eyes wide.

"Did you feel that?" Eddie asked hoarsely.

The first officer swallowed hard. "I thought it was you."

Eddie shook his head. "It wasn't."

The rest of the flight passed in stunned quiet. They landed without further trouble, the wheels kissing the Kansas City runway with almost tender precision. As the passengers disembarked, some weeping with relief, Eddie forced himself to smile, to say the practiced words: "Thank you for flying with us tonight."

But inside, he was reeling.

What had happened in the storm? Had his mind, under pressure, conjured the sensation of another's hands? Had adrenaline lent him strength he didn't know he had? Or had something—someone—taken hold of the plane, steadying it when he could not?

The memory was too sharp, too physical, to dismiss. He knew the difference between muscle strain and a grip not his own.

And he knew this: without that grip, he and every soul aboard would have perished.

That night, long after the passengers had gone home and the plane had been towed into its hangar, Eddie sat alone in his hotel room, staring at his trembling hands.

"They weren't mine," he whispered. "Not mine alone."

And for the first time in decades, the seasoned pilot bowed his head and prayed.

The morning after the storm, Captain Eddie Lawson

looked every bit the professional aviator. Crisp uniform. Polished shoes. Flight bag at his side. But inside, he felt like a man with a secret stitched into his skin.

The airline required a debrief after severe weather encounters. Eddie sat in a small conference room with his first officer, a safety officer, and a manager from operations. Coffee steamed in paper cups. Clipboards waited.

"Walk us through what happened," the safety officer said, pen poised.

Eddie recounted it clinically at first: radar showed storms, turbulence hit, instruments went unreliable, loss of altitude, communication blackout. He stuck to facts, the way a pilot is trained to.

But then came the question he dreaded. Because he knew as a rational man himself how his honest answer would look.

"How did you regain control?"

The room was quiet. Eddie's first officer stared at the table.

Eddie hesitated. He wanted to say *training, instinct, sheer grit.* That would satisfy them, keep him respectable. But another part of him, the part still vibrating with awe, refused to lie.

"I don't think it was me," he said softly.

The safety officer frowned. "What do you mean?"

Eddie met his gaze. "It felt like… someone else had the controls. Like another set of hands. Steadying the plane."

Silence. Then the manager chuckled awkwardly. "You're saying an angel flew the aircraft?"

Eddie flushed. "I'm saying I don't know. But I know I wasn't flying it alone."

The safety officer scribbled something on his clipboard

and quickly shifted the subject. The meeting ended in polite dismissal. But as Eddie left, he caught the sideways glance between the two men: pilot shaken, perhaps not fit for duty.

That was the danger. Pilots were supposed to be calm, rational, masters of the air. There was no room for mystery, no tolerance for anything that hinted at loss of control. Eddie had built his career on being unflappable. And now, if he spoke the truth, he risked being branded unstable.

So he stayed quiet.

Officially, the report listed turbulence and "effective recovery." The passengers were told nothing beyond "unexpected weather." To the outside world, it was another flight that had landed safely thanks to skilled crew.

But Eddie knew better.

At home, he shared the story with his wife, Rosalind.

"I swear, Ros, it wasn't me," he said, pacing the kitchen. "I felt it. Hands on the controls. Stronger than mine. Calm, steady. Like I was just along for the ride."

She studied him carefully. "Are you sure it wasn't adrenaline? You were exhausted, terrified. Maybe your body gave you more strength than you realized. I read about this woman who was able to lift the weight of a car up on her own to free her trapped toddler."

Eddie shook his head fiercely. "I've flown for twenty years. I know what adrenaline feels like. This wasn't that. It was *outside* me. It was… Someone."

Rosalind reached for his hand. "Someone was watching over you, then" she said gently. Her words steadied him more than she knew.

Still, doubt gnawed at him. He replayed the storm in his mind, searching for a rational explanation. Had he unconsciously corrected at the right moment? Had the storm itself shifted? Was the sensation of another grip only a trick of nerves?

But the memory would not blur. It remained sharp, physical, undeniable. He had flown thousands of hours. He knew the feel of controls in his hands. And what he felt that night was not his alone.

The first officer's silence haunted him too. The young man never spoke of it again, never contradicted Eddie outright, but never confirmed it either. Perhaps fear of ridicule kept him quiet. Or perhaps he truly believed it was Eddie's skill. Either way, Eddie knew he could not count on him to corroborate the story.

In the months that followed, Eddie grew cautious about whom he told. He shared it once with a chaplain at the airport, a quiet man who often sat with crew members between flights.

"Do you think God cares enough to guide a plane?" Eddie asked him.

The chaplain smiled. "If He can number the hairs on your head, He can steady an aircraft. Don't you think?"

Eddie chuckled despite himself. "It just feels… too much. Too dramatic."

The chaplain leaned forward. "What's more dramatic than saving two hundred lives?"

Eddie had no answer.

Even as he wrestled with doubt, the experience left a mark. He no longer took flights for granted. Each takeoff carried the memory of that night, the storm, the impossible steadiness. Each landing felt like a gift.

He began praying quietly in the cockpit before flights—not for himself, but for the passengers, the crew, the unseen Presence he now trusted was always near.

He wasn't trying to prove anything anymore. He

simply couldn't forget.

Eddie Lawson had always been defined by competence. Pilots were trained to measure twice, decide once, and never let their passengers sense fear. A pilot's authority was absolute. Yet, after the storm, Eddie carried himself with a new kind of authority—not the stiff confidence of a man in control, but the calm of one who knew control was never entirely his to begin with.

"You're different," Rosalind said one night, studying him across the dinner table.

Eddie only shrugged. "I guess I know now just how fragile it all is. And how much we're carried."

In the cockpit, his change was subtler. He still checked every gauge, followed every procedure. But when storms loomed, he no longer white-knuckled the controls. He flew with a steadier hand, less arrogance, more humility. Co-pilots noticed.

"You don't get rattled," one remarked after a bumpy descent. "Even in turbulence, you're… calm."

Eddie smiled faintly. "I know Who's really flying."

The younger man laughed, assuming it was a joke. Eddie didn't correct him.

Over time, though, Eddie began to share more of the truth. Not with everyone—never in a staff briefing or an official report—but in quiet moments, one-on-one, with those who seemed ready to hear it.

Once, on a layover in Denver, a fellow captain confessed over coffee that he still carried nightmares from a near-crash years before. "Sometimes I wake up drenched in sweat, thinking about the passengers I almost lost," he admitted.

Eddie listened, then said gently, "I know what that's like. But I also know you're not always alone up there.

I've felt it."

And he told the story—carefully, humbly, without embellishment. The other captain's eyes widened, then filled with tears.

The story spread in whispers, pilot to pilot, crew to crew. Eddie never sought it, but he also never denied it when asked. Some scoffed, dismissing it as stress-induced delusion. Others leaned in, hungry for details. A few shared their own accounts: a warning voice in the

He did not trade his captain's stripes for a pulpit. He did not thunder sermons or try to argue skeptics into belief. But in the quiet way he carried himself—in the peace that seemed to settle over him like a second uniform—people sensed something had shifted.

Years later, when Eddie retired, the airline hosted a dinner in his honor. Colleagues toasted his long career, his impeccable safety record, his reputation for calm leadership. Toward the end of the evening, someone asked him to share the secret of his success.

Eddie stood, glass in hand, and paused. He could have spoken about training, discipline, teamwork. Instead, he said quietly:

"The truth is, I was never flying alone. None of us are."

Reflection — Hands on the Yoke

Air travel is built on control. Charts, gauges, checklists, calculations—every aspect is designed to leave as little to chance as possible. Pilots are trained to believe that mastery of their machines will keep them safe. Yet Eddie Lawson's story reminds us that even the most seasoned aviator meets the limits of his strength. And in those moments, something beyond skill may break through.

The skeptic can object easily. The brain under stress does strange things. Muscles twitch. Perceptions warp. Perhaps Eddie misread his own body, felt a phantom pressure, convinced himself of help because he could not bear the thought of failure. These explanations sound tidy, respectable.

But they do not erase the fruit of the experience. Eddie did not emerge shattered, unstable, unfit. He emerged calmer, humbler, more certain that his life—and the lives of those entrusted to him—rested not solely in his hands but in larger ones. That is not madness. That is transformation.

At its heart, his story is not about aviation but about surrender. About what happens when we discover that our strength is not enough, that the storm is bigger than our training, that the instruments spin uselessly and the sky itself turns hostile. For some, that realization breeds despair. For others, like Eddie, it opens a door.

He had spent two decades defining himself by competence. But in the storm, competence broke. And when it did, grace entered—not in a sermon, not in a vision, but in the tangible feel of another's grip steadying his own.

It was not proof in a scientific sense. It was assurance in a human sense. Assurance that he was not alone. Assurance that surrender is not the same as defeat.

How many of us live the same way—white-knuckling our days, convinced that survival depends entirely on our grip? We plot, plan, fight, strain, refusing to admit that we cannot hold it all together. And yet, again and again, life proves otherwise. The storms come. The controls slip. The spin begins.

Eddie's story offers a different image: hands layered over ours, strong where we are weak, calm where we are frantic. Guidance that does not erase responsibility—we still hold the yoke—but steadies it with a strength not our own.

That image can reframe more than flying. It can reframe living.

Perhaps this is why Eddie chose not to argue his story into credibility. He never insisted others believe. He simply bore witness: *I wasn't flying alone.* And that quiet testimony became enough.

Testimony 4
In The Line of Fire

The desert night was alive with sound. Not the quiet kind of crickets and wind, but the sharp, violent staccato of war: gunfire rattling, mortars thudding, the crack of explosions echoing off concrete walls. Private First Class Aaron Radcliffe crouched low in the rubble of a half-collapsed building on the outskirts of Fallujah, Iraq, his breath shallow, his rifle trembling in his hands.

It was supposed to be a routine patrol. Their squad had rolled out just after sundown, Humvees rumbling through narrow streets, headlights cutting across shuttered windows. The intel was sketchy—insurgents in the area, maybe planning an ambush. Nothing unusual. Nothing they hadn't faced before.

But then the first shot rang out. Then another. In seconds, the street was an inferno of bullets, RPGs streaking fire through the dark. The squad scattered for cover. Aaron dove through the jagged opening of the ruined building, landing hard, ears ringing.

He had been in firefights before, but this one was different. It was relentless, unyielding, like the city itself had risen against them. The squad radio crackled with panic. A Humvee was hit. One of his friends was down. The night became a blur of shouting, shooting, praying, bleeding.

Pinned in the rubble, Aaron felt certain he was about to die.

He gripped his rifle so tightly his knuckles ached. "God," he whispered, his voice lost in the roar of battle, "please don't let me die here. Not *here*."

And then—like a switch thrown—the chaos around him seemed to shift.

Not that the bullets stopped. Not that the mortars fell silent. But something changed in the air. A stillness. A presence. As if time itself had slowed down.

Aaron could not see it the way he saw the muzzle flashes in the street. He could not hear it the way he heard his comrades' frantic voices. But he *felt* it, as real as the rubble pressing into his side: a nearness, a shield, a weight of protection that wrapped around him like unseen armor.

Bullets struck the walls inches from his head. Dust rained down, sharp fragments of concrete stinging his face. But none touched him. He should have been hit a dozen times. But he wasn't.

At one point, he risked a glance over the wall—and swore he saw a figure standing in the haze, luminous even in the smoky dark. It was gone in a blink, but the impression stayed: tall, steady, calm. Watching. Guarding.

Hours blurred. The firefight raged, but Aaron moved with a strange confidence, darting across alleys, pulling a wounded friend to cover, firing with precision that surprised even himself. Fear had not left him—it pounded in his chest with every heartbeat—but beneath the fear was something deeper. A certainty: *You are not alone.*

Finally, near dawn, reinforcements arrived. The insurgents melted into the city. Silence fell, heavy and exhausted.

When the squad regrouped, battered and bloodied, Aaron realized with shock that he was unscathed. His uniform was torn. His helmet dented. But his body—every inch of it—was intact.

A fellow soldier clapped him on the shoulder. "Man, you must have nine lives. I saw the rounds hitting all around you."

Aaron could only nod, too stunned to speak. He knew it wasn't luck.

Later, back at base, as he scrubbed dust from his skin and tried to steady his hands, Aaron replayed the night in his mind. The figure in the haze. The shield around him. The impossible fact that he had walked through fire and emerged untouched.

He whispered into the stillness of his bunk, "Thank You."

It was the only prayer he could manage.

The hours after combat were always the hardest. The adrenaline bled away, leaving only exhaustion and the sour taste of fear. Men who had roared in battle now sat silent, staring at nothing, their hands still trembling from the weight of rifles.

Aaron Radcliffe sat on his bunk in the dim barracks, boots half-unlaced, uniform streaked with soot. He had cleaned his weapon mechanically, as every soldier did, but his mind was miles away. The firefight replayed itself in fragments: the flash of RPGs, the thud of mortars, the friend he had dragged by his vest through a hail of bullets. And always, the same impossible detail: how none of it had touched him.

He lifted his hands in the dim light. They were whole. His body was whole. He should have been carried out in a body bag. Instead, here he was, alive.

The memory of that presence pulsed in him. He had felt it as surely as he felt the ground under his boots. A shield. A guardian. Something beyond reason.

And yet… doubt pressed in. Had it been adrenaline? A trick of terror, his brain conjuring comfort where none existed? Had the figure in the haze been smoke and imagination?

Aaron dropped his head into his hands. "I don't know," he whispered to himself to answer his own question. "But I know I'm alive."

The next morning, the squad gathered in the mess hall. The atmosphere was subdued. Three soldiers had been injured, one seriously. The losses weighed heavy, though every man tried to wear the mask of toughness.

"You're one lucky b---, Radcliffe," Sergeant Miller muttered over his coffee. "I saw the rounds bouncing off that wall like popcorn. Don't know how you didn't catch one."

Aaron forced a smile. "Neither do I."

Another soldier, Diaz, leaned across the table. "Luck, hell. You had someone watching your six. My grandma always said we got guardian angels." He pointed his spoon at Aaron. "Yours must've been working overtime."

The table erupted in chuckles, half-joking, half-serious as Aaron nodded slowly. Aaron laughed too, but inside his chest, the words struck deep. *Guardian angel.* It was the closest anyone had come to naming what he felt.

Later, in private, one of the wounded men he had dragged to safety pulled him close.

"You saved my life out there," Corporal Davis rasped, his side wrapped in bandages. "But don't tell me it was just you. Something else was with us. I swear, when you grabbed me, I felt… peace. Warmth. Right in the middle of that nightmare."

Aaron stared at him. "You felt it too?"

Davis nodded. "Yeah. Like we weren't alone."

The conversation left Aaron shaken. He wasn't the only one.

"Why us?"

Davis could only shrug his shoulders. Many a good man had fallen in Fallujah. But that something supernatural had intervened for them was undeniable.

Still, not everyone was so open. When Aaron tentatively shared with another friend what he had seen—the luminous figure in the haze—the friend frowned.

"You were stressed. Seeing things. Happens all the time in combat."

Aaron bristled. "I wasn't hallucinating."

"Then what was it? God Himself walking around Fallujah?" The soldier shook his head. "Think you're so special for God to send his flippy flappy angels in just for you, huh? Come on, man, get a grip!"

Aaron had no answer. He only knew he couldn't dismiss it as readily as the naysayers. He was grateful Davis had sensed the presence too – it kept him from using his soldier logic to write the experience off as imagination or misremembering Even while it was precisely because of his soldier training that he had observed and recalled in such vivid detail.

Nights stretched long. Sleep was broken, haunted by dreams of smoke and gunfire. But woven through the nightmares was that same unshakable impression of protection, like a hand resting on his shoulder.

One night, unable to sleep, Aaron opened the small Bible his mother had tucked into his pack before he deployed. He hadn't touched it in months. The pages smelled faintly of home, of her perfume.

His eyes fell on Psalm 91: *"He will cover you with his feathers, and under his wings you will find refuge. His faithfulness will be your shield and rampart."*

Aaron closed his eyes. The words felt less like poetry and more like description.

Weeks passed. The war ground on. Patrols continued. But Aaron was not the same soldier who had crouched in terror in the rubble. Something had shifted.

He still fought, still carried his rifle, still faced the chaos. But now he carried something else too: the memory of being shielded, inexplicably, unmistakably, in the valley of death.

He didn't talk about it often. He wasn't sure he could. But deep inside, he carried a certainty that could not be argued away:

I was not alone.

War changes everyone. Some men hardened. Some grew reckless, daring death to catch them. Others collapsed under the weight of trauma, unable to shake the echoes of explosions and cries. Aaron Radcliffe carried his own scars—nights when the gunfire still rang in his ears, days when sudden noises made him flinch—but he also carried something else, something rare: a quiet assurance that he had been held in the fire.

It didn't make him fearless. It made him different.

Back on patrol, his squad noticed the shift first. Where before he had been jittery, cautious to the point of hesitation, now he moved with a steadiness that surprised them. He still ducked when bullets flew, still fought for his life like any man would—but beneath it all was calm.

"You're ice, Radcliffe," Sergeant Miller remarked after one firefight. "What changed?"

Aaron shrugged. He couldn't explain it without

sounding crazy. Finally, he said simply, "I just know I'm not out there alone."

Miller raised an eyebrow but said nothing more.

The shift showed in other ways too. He began checking in more on his fellow soldiers, offering quiet encouragement, a hand on the shoulder, a word at the right time. He pulled men back from recklessness, spoke steadying words when panic threatened to unravel them. He wasn't the loudest or the toughest in the unit, but somehow the others gravitated toward him.

Diaz called him "Preach," half-joking. But the nickname stuck.

Aaron didn't preach in the pulpit sense. He didn't give speeches or sermons. But when a man sat beside him in the dark, whispering about fear, or when someone asked why he always carried that little Bible in his pack now, Aaron would tell just enough of his story.

"I should've been dead that night," he would say. "But something—someone—shielded me. You can laugh if you want, but I believe it was real."

Some did laugh. Others nodded solemnly. A few were hungry for more.

When his deployment ended and Aaron returned home, the adjustment was jarring. The streets were too quiet, the colors too bright, the routines of civilian life too simple after the raw intensity of war. He carried the weight of things he'd seen—friends lost, civilians caught in crossfire, wounds that no medal could cover.

But he also carried the memory of that night in Fallujah. The presence. The shield. The figure in the haze.

He poured it into his life. With his wife, he was gentler, more attentive. With his children, when they came later, he was patient in a way his own father had never been.

He started volunteering at the VA, sitting with other veterans, listening to their stories, sometimes sharing his own.

Many were haunted by nightmares, by guilt, by the sense that war had taken something from them that could never be restored. Aaron never dismissed their pain. He knew it too. But he would lean forward and say, "I don't know why I walked out alive when others didn't. But I know I wasn't alone. And I don't think you are either."

Over the years, the story became less about what he saw and more about how he lived. He didn't insist on angels or visions. He didn't debate skeptics. He simply bore witness through the steadiness of his presence, the peace he carried, the way he leaned toward others instead of away. Friends and neighbors knew him as a man of quiet faith, a soldier who had walked through fire and come back with something unburned inside him.

When asked directly, he would still describe that night. The bullets, the shield, the figure. "You can call it what you want," he'd say with a faint smile. "But I call it mercy."

His children grew up hearing fragments of the story, pieced together over time. They noticed how he prayed before meals, how he folded Psalm 91 into their bedtime routines, how he never let a day go by without gratitude.

"Daddy," his daughter asked once, "were you scared?"

He pulled her close. "Terrified, Honey," he said honestly. "But I wasn't alone. That's what made the difference."

And though he never sought attention, his testimony had a way of rippling outward—changing the lives of those who heard it, reminding them that even in the darkest battles, there can be a Presence no bullet can pierce.

Reflection — A Shield in Battle

War has a way of stripping life down to its rawest edges. It shows us how fragile the body is, how quickly breath can vanish, how thin the line between life and death really runs. It also exposes the limits of human strength. Training, discipline, courage—they all matter. But even the bravest soldier eventually meets a moment when skill is not enough.

Aaron Radcliffe's tale inhabits that uncertain space—where bullets rip through the sky, where logic screams that survival is beyond reach, where fear devours any glimmer of hope. Yet, in that harrowing place, he sensed something far beyond himself. A force. A shield. A presence. A guardian watching over him.

Skeptics will say it was adrenaline, chance, or the selective memory of trauma. Perhaps. But even skeptics must account for what followed. Aaron did not come home hardened or embittered. He came home gentler, steadier, marked not only by the horrors of war but by a peace that endured. Peace is not the fruit of hallucination. Peace is the fruit of presence.

The Bible speaks often of God as a shield. Abraham heard the words: *"Do not be afraid, Abram. I am your shield, your very great reward"* (Genesis 15:1). The psalmist declared, *"You are my hiding place; you will protect me from trouble and surround me with songs of deliverance"* (Psalm 32:7). These images are not abstract—they are rooted in the lived experience of people who had walked through danger and found themselves preserved.

Aaron's account sits in continuity with that long testimony: *I should have been destroyed. I was not. I was not alone.*

Davis' life also changed dramatically. Working now as a first responder in California, he has been used to save many lives.

There is a temptation in war stories to glorify violence, to turn battles into theater and survival into victory. Aaron resisted that. He never claimed that God chose sides in a human conflict, never painted his experience as a weapon against another faith. What he knew was simpler, humbler: that in the chaos, mercy had encircled him.

That distinction matters. Because it reframes the testimony not as triumphalism but as grace. Not "we were right and they were wrong," but "I was spared when I could not spare myself."

For those who have never worn a uniform, Aaron's story still speaks. Because though few of us will crouch under fire in Fallujah, all of us know what it is to be pinned down by life—by grief, fear, uncertainty, loss. We know what it feels like when the air is thick with danger, when the walls seem to close in, when survival feels unlikely.

And in those moments, what we most need is what Aaron discovered: the assurance of presence. The sense—sometimes faint, sometimes overwhelming—that we are not abandoned. That even in fire, there is a shield.

Of course, we cannot always explain why one is spared and another is not. Aaron himself carried that burden: the question of why he walked out whole when others did not. Scripture does not give easy answers to such mysteries. But it does give testimony, again and again, that God is near to the broken, that He commands His angels concerning His people, that no darkness is beyond His reach.

And perhaps that is enough. Not an explanation, but a promise. Not a map of why, but a witness to who.

Aaron's life became that kind of witness. Not flashy. Not loud. But steady, like the shield he had felt that night. A quiet reminder to his family, his friends, his fellow veterans that there is a Presence no bullet can pierce, no storm can scatter, no darkness can erase.

His story is not an argument. It is an invitation. To wonder. To hope. To trust that we are not as alone as we fear.

Testimony 5
The Voice in the Car

Let's talk about divine intervention—because if you think guardian angels clock out after childhood, buckle up. Some miracles don't come swathed in ethereal light or floating on harp music. Sometimes, they sound like a stranger's voice screaming through shattered glass, barking orders in the split second between life and death.

One second. One command. One breath between "I'm dead" and "I'm alive."

That's all it takes.

A truck's brake lights screaming toward you.

A doctor's shrug before the scan reveals the inexplicable.

A stranger who vanishes after pulling you from flames —*no footprints left in the snow.*

You won't find these stories in stained glass. You'll find them in ER waiting rooms, in the shaky laughter of survivors, in the quiet of a hospital chapel where someone whispers, *"That wasn't just luck."*

Angels don't always announce themselves.

But when they do?

You'll *know.*

Sheila Hammond had never thought of herself as the sort of person who would end up in a book about angels. She was, by her own admission, "painfully ordinary." A schoolteacher in her forties, she lived in a modest home on the edge of town, paid her bills on time, and tried to keep her roses alive despite the stubborn clay soil in her garden. Her faith, too, was ordinary — church on Sundays, hymns sung half a tone too flat, whispered prayers before sleep more out of habit than burning conviction.

If anything, she would have described herself as cautious. She drove under the speed limit. She disliked flying. She preferred routines to surprises. Even her friends teased her gently: "Sheila, you'd never be the heroine of an adventure novel." And she would laugh, relieved, because adventure sounded far too dangerous.

But it was precisely this cautious, ordinary woman who found herself standing at the very edge of disaster, only to be pulled back by an extraordinary voice that could not be explained.

It was a late summer evening, the kind that still carried the day's warmth but hinted of autumn in the breeze. Sheila had stayed late at school, grading essays, and by the time she packed her bag, the car park was already deserted. She drove home on the back roads, enjoying the quiet, her mind wandering through lesson plans and the half-forgotten groceries she ought to pick up.

A storm was brewing in the distance. She noticed it first as a smudge of grey on the horizon, then as flashes of light that pulsed faintly behind the clouds. The radio crackled with weather warnings — sudden downpours, high winds, localized flooding. Sheila frowned, gripping the wheel tighter. She disliked storms almost as much as she disliked surprises.

The first drops of rain splattered her windshield just as she turned onto a rural stretch of road bordered by fields. Within minutes, the drizzle became a deluge.

Wipers swiped furiously, barely keeping pace. Thunder rolled overhead, closer now, rattling the air.

Sheila leaned forward, squinting through the blur. She knew this road well; it crossed a bridge over a creek notorious for flooding in heavy rain. But the bridge was solid - had been standing there decades - longer than she'd been alive - and had survived worse weather than this. Sheila pressed on slowly, heart thudding as she neared the bridge.

The storm was deafening — rain hammering the roof, wind buffeting the car, thunder cracking so loud it seemed to shake her bones. The bridge loomed ahead.

And then, cutting through the chaos, came a voice. Not a whisper. Not a thought. An audible *command*, a man's voice clear as a bell: *"Stop. Now."*

Muscle memory met divine intervention. No hesitation. No second-guessing. Sheila's body moved before her mind could question why she was hearing a man's voice inside her car, let alone one telling her to stop She slammed the brake pedal, tires screeching as the car skidded to a halt just meters before the bridge.

In the next second, the world shifted.

The bridge, already slick with water, groaned and gave way. With a sound like a tree snapping, the central section collapsed into the torrent below. Had she taken even two more seconds, she would have been on it. She would have gone down with it.

Sheila gripped the steering wheel, trembling. Rain battered the windshield, but she barely noticed. All she could hear was the echo of that voice: *Stop. Now.*

She was alive because of it.

She sat motionless for minutes, pulse racing, as water roared below the broken bridge. She looked about her but there was nobody there. Seemingly no one for miles.

And besides, the voice had been as if the speaker was right inside the vehicle. The noise of the rain pelting off the roads was so loud in any case that she would not have heard anyone shout outside her vehicle in any case. Every instinct told her to explain it away — but deep down, she knew better. The timing was too precise, the tone too foreign. It had not been her own thoughts.

It had been something — someone — else. Something supernatural.

Finally, shaking, she reversed slowly and found another route home. By the time she stumbled into her house, soaked and pale, she could barely speak. When at last she did, it was only a whisper: “Thank You.”

She did not know who she was thanking exactly. But she knew she had not been alone.

For days afterward, Sheila could not shake the sound of that voice. It replayed in her mind at odd moments: while she stood at the sink washing dishes, while she scribbled notes on lesson plans, even in the middle of conversations. Always the same words, always the same tone — urgent, commanding, unlike anything she had ever heard before.

Stop. Now.

At first she told no one. How could she? To say out loud that she had heard a disembodied voice in a storm was to invite raised eyebrows, awkward silences, or gentle suggestions about stress. And Sheila, cautious as ever, dreaded the thought of becoming the subject of whispers in the staffroom - or worse, the playground.

So she carried the secret quietly. She replayed the event again and again in her mind, trying to find a natural explanation even while fully understanding there was none.

Perhaps she had seen the bridge sagging through the

rain without realizing it, her subconscious registering the danger before her conscious mind caught up. Perhaps her own internal alarm had taken the shape of a voice. She had read somewhere that under extreme stress, the brain could manufacture vivid sensory impressions. Perhaps it was precognition - but the voice.

The voice - apart from being male - had not sounded like her. Her own thoughts were hesitant, questioning, full of qualifiers. This voice had been certain. Commanding. It had spoken with an authority that brooked no hesitation. And it had come not half a second too early, not half a second too late, but at the exact instant needed to save her life.

The more she turned it over, the more she realized: explanation was thinner than testimony.

A week later, she found herself blurting it out to her sister, Margaret, over tea.

"I… something happened to me the other night."

Margaret looked up from her cup, concerned. "Are you all right?"

"Yes. Well, I am. But I shouldn't be. I was driving home in the storm, and just before I crossed the old bridge… it collapsed, Maggie. Right in front of me. I should have been on it. A few seconds and—"

Margaret gasped. "Sheila! That's terrible. You could have—"

"I know. But that's not the strangest part." Sheila lowered her voice, embarrassed. "I stopped the car because I heard a voice. It said, 'Stop. Now.' Clear as anything. A man's voice as if beside me in my vehicle. And if I hadn't listened…" She trailed off, eyes brimming.

Silence stretched between them for a moment. Margaret reached out and took her hand. "Sheila…

maybe it was your guardian angel."

Sheila almost laughed in relief and protest at once even though she could not deny that was exactly what she had been considering. "Do you really think so? I mean, that sounds like something out of a children's Bible story."

Margaret squeezed her hand. "Why not? You're alive, aren't you?"

The idea unsettled Sheila more than it comforted her. Guardian angels belonged in Sunday school illustrations, not in the life of a middle-aged teacher with roses that refused to bloom. She had never thought herself particularly holy or worthy of special attention. Why should heaven bother with her?

And yet the evidence stared her in the face every time she drove past the bridge, now cordoned off with yellow tape. She could not escape the fact: something — someone — had spoken to her.

Her pastor was the next to hear. After church one Sunday, when most had left and the sanctuary echoed only with the sound of hymnals closing, she lingered awkwardly. Finally she approached him, words tumbling out.

He listened without interruption, his lined face calm. When she finished, flushing with self-consciousness, he said simply, "Sheila, I believe you."

"You do?"

"I've heard such stories before. Rare, yes. But not unheard of. God sometimes sends His messengers to protect His people. Sometimes they appear in visible form. Sometimes, just their voices are heard."

Sheila blinked back tears. "But why me? I'm not important. I'm not…" She gestured helplessly.

The pastor smiled. "Importance has nothing to do

with it. God's care is not rationed to the worthy. He knows every hair on your head. He knew you needed to hear those words in that moment. That's enough."

Still, doubt lingered. Sheila found herself oscillating between wonder and skepticism. Some days she whispered thanks with trembling certainty. Other days she scolded herself for fanciful thinking. Yet beneath it all, one fact remained immovable: she was alive because she had obeyed a voice that should not have been there.

And slowly, quietly, that fact began to reshape her.

She prayed more often, not out of habit but out of genuine conversation. She lingered over Scripture with fresh curiosity, especially the passages about angels. She noticed how often in the Bible they spoke with words of command: to Lot fleeing Sodom, to Philip sent down a desert road, to Joseph warned in dreams, to the women at the empty tomb. Always short, always urgent, always clear.

She realized her own experience fit the pattern.

And with that realization came a shift. She was no longer merely a woman who had survived a storm. She was a witness to something greater.

Months passed. The storm faded into ordinary weather reports, the bridge was rebuilt and reopened, life moved on — but the voice lingered. She carried it like a stone in her pocket: always there, always pressing against her awareness.

At first she tried to keep it private. But testimonies have a way of pressing outward. Little by little, the story slipped from her lips — at her church, with friends, once even in the staffroom at school when colleagues were swapping tales of close calls.

Most nodded politely, unsure what to say. A few looked skeptical, though they tried to hide it. One teacher quipped, "Well, at least your subconscious has good timing!" The others chuckled, and Sheila forced a smile, but inside she felt the old tug of doubt. Was that all it was?

And yet, when she retold the story in quieter company, she saw a different reaction. One evening at a prayer group, after hesitant confession, an elderly woman leaned forward, eyes shining. "My dear, something similar happened to me once. I was about to step off a curb when a voice told me to stop. A lorry thundered past not a second later. I never told anyone until now, for fear of being thought crazy."

The room fell silent, reverent. Sheila realized she was not alone. Others, too, had brushed against the mystery.

The more she shared, the more the story began to shape her identity. She was no longer merely Sheila the teacher, Sheila the cautious, Sheila the ordinary. She was Sheila who had heard a voice. Sheila who had been spared. Sheila who bore witness to something greater than herself. Despite her ordinariness.

At times the weight of it felt heavy. Why had she been saved when others were not? That question haunted her most when news reports carried stories of lives lost in floods, storms, accidents. Families mourning loved ones who had not heard a voice in their moment of danger. Why her?

Her pastor's words echoed: *importance has nothing to do with it.* Still, she wrestled.

The wrestling did not drive her from faith; it deepened it. She learned to sit with mystery rather than demand answers. She came to see her experience not as proof of divine favoritism but as a signpost — a reminder that God sees, God cares, God sometimes intervenes.

That was 1978. Years later, Sheila would retell the

story to her great nieces and nephews. By then, the storm had become a family legend, one the children begged to hear. "Tell us about the bridge!" they would plead, eyes wide.

She would settle into her chair, smile softly, and recount it once again: the rain, the voice, the sudden collapse. Always ending with the same words: "I am alive because someone told me to stop. I believe it was an angel, sent by God to protect me."

The children would listen in awe, then pepper her with questions. "Did you see the angel? Was it a man or a woman? Did you hear the voice again?"

Sheila would shake her head. "No. I didn't see anyone. And I never heard the voice again."

In time, those children would tell their friends, who would tell others, and the testimony rippled outward. What had once embarrassed her became her legacy. With the assurance that the same God in 1978 was alive in 1988, 1998, 2008, 2018…

And every time she drove across a bridge, no matter how solid, no matter how clear the weather, she whispered a prayer of thanks. Not because she lived in fear, but because she lived with gratitude. Every span of road became a reminder of the night when heaven's voice broke through the storm.

Reflection — When Heaven Speaks

Sheila Hammond's story reminds us that not all angelic encounters arrive in visible form. Sometimes heaven does not step into the room with blinding light or radiant figures. Sometimes it speaks. A voice in the storm. A word in the moment of decision. A command that saves.

Her testimony carries echoes of Scripture. Angels have spoken throughout the biblical story, and their words are nearly always short, sharp, and decisive. To Lot in Sodom: *"Get up! Take your wife and your daughters… or you will be swept away."* To Hagar in the wilderness: *"Do not be afraid."* To Philip in Samaria: *"Go south to the desert road."* To Joseph in dreams: *"Take the child and his mother and flee."* Always urgent, always clear, always precise. Not philosophical discourses, not long explanations — just words tailored to the need of the moment.

That is exactly what Sheila experienced. No preamble. No comfort speech. Simply: *Stop. Now.* And that was enough.

Skeptics will say she heard her own subconscious. That adrenaline sharpened her perception, that her brain invented a voice to jolt her into action. And perhaps there are times when that is true. The human mind is capable of remarkable instincts under pressure. But when testimony presses beyond instinct — when the words are crisp, commanding, distinct from the usual cadence of one's own thoughts — then perhaps we are standing on holy ground.

For Sheila, the difference was unmistakable. She knew her own hesitations, her own cautious inner monologue. This was not that. This was authority that brooked no delay. And the proof lay in timing: had she paused to question it, she would have been lost.

There is something humbling about this. Sheila was not a missionary in prison, not a martyr at the stake, not a prophet on a mountaintop. She was an ordinary schoolteacher, cautious, timid, "painfully ordinary," as she put it. And yet heaven bent low enough to warn her.

That is grace. God does not ration His care to the extraordinary. He does not reserve His messengers for the saints whose names fill history books. He knows the hairs on the head of every believer. He knows the fragile lives of those we call ordinary. And sometimes, when needed most, He sends a voice.

The challenge is not to explain such stories, but to receive them. They will never satisfy scientific curiosity. They were not given for that purpose. They were given to protect, to guide, to remind. Their fruit is not in argument but in gratitude. Sheila emerged with a deeper awareness that she was not alone, that her life was held, that God's care extended even to her cautious, (to her) unremarkable path.

And that awareness reshaped her. Prayer became conversation. Scripture became alive. Gratitude became her posture. Witness became her legacy.

This, too, is the fruit of angelic voices in Scripture. Hagar named the Lord as *"the God who sees me."* Joseph obeyed without delay, protecting the child entrusted to him. Philip went to the desert road, where a single Ethiopian soul awaited the gospel. The voice did not end in itself; it propelled lives into deeper obedience and trust.

So with Sheila. And that, in the end, is the true measure of heavenly encounters — not how dramatic they are, but how they shape the witness of those who receive them.

And what of us? Few will hear such a voice - audibly, at least. Many will wish for it in times of confusion and danger. But even if heaven does not speak audibly, God has not left us without guidance. His Word is living and active. His Spirit whispers conviction. His people speak truth in love. And sometimes, in moments of urgency, those voices come with a weight that feels otherworldly.

Perhaps the challenge is not whether we will hear a

voice, but whether we will obey it when it comes - however it comes.

Sheila's story reminds us that God's care extends into storms and creeks and back roads as much as into pulpits and prisons. It reminds us that the unseen is never far away, even from the most ordinary lives. And it invites us to live attentive, listening, ready to obey when the whisper - or shout - comes.

When Heaven Shouts

Angels don't always fit the Hallmark card aesthetic—soft-focus, wings spread, gently strumming harps. Sometimes, they appear as a barked order in your ear when the semi-truck drifts into your lane. A shout in the chaos, a supernatural GPS rerouting you from disaster. A gut punch of instinct that's too precise, too *timely* to be yours alone.

I've heard these stories for decades now.

- The man who swears someone *yanked* his steering wheel to avoid black ice—then found no one in the passenger seat.
- The woman whose friend, halfway across the world in England, who while in the half state between sleep and wakefulness had heard a man's voice warn her: *"I know this sounds crazy... but I had to warn you. Don't eat breakfast in the car today."* (She avoided a four-car pileup because her hands were able to rapidly react on the wheel.)
- The mother who heard *"BRAKE NOW"* seconds before her toddler darted into the street.

Psalm 91:11 isn't poetry—it's a battle plan.

"He will command His angels concerning you..."

Command. Not suggest. Not hope. *Command.*

Sheila didn't pray for rescue that morning. Didn't "deserve" it more than anyone else on the road. Grace doesn't work like that. It's the unearned, undignified, *unmistakable* shout in your darkest moment—the one that leaves you breathless in the aftermath, staring at the wreckage of what *should have been* and whispering:

"That wasn't me."

Here's the truth:

The same God who parted the Red Sea still reroutes ambulances.

The same voice that woke Samuel in the temple now shouts through shattered windshields.

And the love that numbered the hairs on your head? It counts the seconds between you and disaster—then steps in.

So the next time you walk away from the near-miss, the almost-catastrophe, the *how-was-that-not-worse...*

Pause.

Listen.

And thank the One who sent the angel you didn't see—but absolutely heard.

These aren't coincidences. They're receipts.

The Unseen Battalion: A Benediction for the Almost-Disasters

Make no mistake—

Angels still clock in.

They ride shotgun in your Honda.

They loiter near your child's crib.

They murmur in languages your spirit understands

before your brain catches up.

Turn here.

Slow down.

Wake up.

Look again.

So when you walk away from the close call—hands shaking, heart pounding—don't just shrug it off as luck.

Stand still for a moment.

Let the gratitude rise up like incense.

And know this:

The same God who kept Sheila Hammond alive?

He's still writing those kinds of stories.

And friend?

You're in one.

Because the truth is, angels are still on assignment.

Testimony 6, 7 & 8
The Underground Church

In some places, churches exist with government permission—but under tight surveillance, their sermons censored, their loyalty to the state demanded above all. Yet for countless believers, the true church gathers elsewhere: in dimly lit apartments, hidden basements, the back rooms of shops after closing. They meet in hushed tones, ears straining for the sudden knock at the door, hearts braced for interruption.

For them, faith is not a Sunday ritual but a daily gamble. To follow Christ is to sign, in invisible ink, a covenant of suffering. Arrests. Beatings. Interrogations. Fines that leave families destitute. Years behind bars. And still, they come. They gather., They whisper hymns, pass well-worn pages of Scripture between trembling hands, and pray—for courage, for their persecutors—echoing the ancient cry of the church: "We must obey God rather than men."

It was in such hidden spaces that stories began to surface—stories whispered between believers, shared with tears and trembling. Stories of doors that would not break down though police rammed them. Stories of interrogators frozen mid-step. Stories of light in darkness, of figures standing guard, of the sense of presence so thick it filled the room like incense.

Some dismiss them as rumor, exaggeration born of

fear. Yet I cannot. For I have sat across wooden tables with believers who told them in halting voices, not for spectacle but as testimony. I've seen the way their eyes shone with memory, not invention. And I carry my own memories too from the years when I slipped Bibles across borders, back when the Iron Curtain still divided Europe.

Those were dangerous days. A wrong step at a checkpoint meant prison or worse. I remember sweating under the gaze of uniformed guards, praying silently as they searched my vehicle. More than once, I felt the atmosphere shift in a way I could not explain — a guard suddenly distracted, a suitcase left unopened, a sense that Someone unseen had drawn near. And once, I sensed I met an angel in the flesh -—not radiant, not winged, but an ordinary-looking young man with an extraordinary presence. He appeared beside us as I gave witness to Christ outside a communist headquarters, and suddenly, my words burned with an unearthly power. A literal weight pressed upon my tongue; my voice rang bold. Four souls turned to faith that day, as if the man's presence had unleashed an anointing on my words. Then, as swiftly as he came, he vanished.

So I listen to these accounts from China's underground church—not as a skeptic nor a credulous collector of tales, but as one who has tasted heaven's nearness. And what moves me most is this: heaven reveals itself to both the faithful and the faithless. To the believer clinging to hope. And to the persecutor, the unwitting pawn of oppression, who stumbles upon what he cannot explain.

That dual witness is important. Too often, angel stories are confined to the inner circle of the already convinced, told and retold as encouragement. But when the persecutor himself becomes a witness, when the man trained to mock faith stumbles into mystery — that is a different kind of testimony altogether. It disarms excuses. It leaves skeptics with fewer places to hide.

So here, together, are two stories from China. One angel told through the eyes of a man who did not believe. The other angel through the eyes of one who did. Two perspectives, two encounters, two different occasions: one thread: that in the crucible of persecution, heaven sometimes makes itself unavoidably present.

And I will say this before we begin: these are not isolated anecdotes. In my travels, I have heard dozens like them — from house churches in Henan, from gatherings in Shanghai, from whispered testimonies in rural villages where faith is still branded a crime. I have heard them from pastors who were beaten, from grandmothers who smuggled hymn sheets under their coats, from young men who spent years in prison yet emerged with faces shining like Moses from the mountain. The pattern is undeniable. The persecuted often see what the comfortable rarely do.

Perhaps that is part of the mystery: when the world strips you of protection, heaven's nearness becomes harder to miss. When power threatens to crush you, Presence sometimes pushes back.

These two stories —of the unbeliever and the believer —are not offered as arguments, nor as entertainment. They are offered as witness. You may choose skepticism, searching for rational explanations. You may decide the brain invents visions under stress. But at least allow yourself this: to hear what was seen and remembered, and to consider whether the unseen world is closer than we dare believe.

China Story A - The Believer's side

Faith, when hidden, often burns brightest. While some worship in cathedrals and chapels, others gather in basements, apartments, or back rooms, their voices lowered, their eyes watchful, their songs rising in whispers rather than shouts.

Jun Chao was one of them. He was, on the surface, a model citizen of modern China. He was the only son of a Communist Party official, bright, well-educated, and working comfortably as a software engineer. Outwardly, he lived the life expected of him: good job, good family connections, good prospects.

But Jun had a secret. Some evenings, instead of heading straight home after work, he parked his car near a busy restaurant and slipped away on foot. He wasn't sneaking off to gamble or drink — his "vice" was far more dangerous. He was attending an underground house church.

He moved with practiced precision—changing subway lines three times, doubling back through crowded shopping districts, finally disappearing into a maze of narrow alleyways in an unremarkable residential quarter.

His destination was a fourth-floor apartment where a dozen believers gathered in violation of half a dozen laws. They came in ones and twos, entering through the back stairwell after giving the correct coded knock. Inside, the air hummed with whispered prayers and the scent of jasmine tea, the windows carefully covered

Every aspect of their gathering had been engineered for survival. Members arrived and departed in carefully staggered intervals. A designated watchman monitored police frequencies on a hacked radio. The location changed weekly, rotating through a network of trusted homes. The risk was unimaginable—discovery meant not just prison, but potential "re-education" for entire families, the erasure of careers, the unraveling of generations of social standing.

Yet Jun Chao kept returning..

It had begun with a single gospel tract slipped inside a pirated programming manual—a flimsy pamphlet that should have angered him. But the words had lodged in his mind like shrapnel: *"For God so loved the world..."* Late at night, in the privacy of his high-rise apartment, he found himself searching for more. The answers led him down digital rabbit holes, to encrypted forums, and eventually to Brother Wang, who met him in a public park and spoke of a love greater than fear.

Their first meeting took place in a crowded Starbucks, Wang posing as a business contact. When the older man slid a microSD card across the table containing the complete Bible, Jun's hands shook so badly he nearly dropped it.

For weeks, their Bible studies happened in moving cars, Starbucks, the back rooms of karaoke bars—anywhere the surveillance nets had blind spots. Jun Chao drank in Scripture like a man dying of thirst, each verse dismantling another pillar of his Communist indoctrination. The night he finally prayed to receive Christ as his personal Lord and Saviour, he and Wang and another brother stood waist-deep in the Yangtze River at 3 AM, the dark waters swallowing his tears of repentance.

Now, Jun Chao ascended the dim stairwell with measured steps, each creak of the aging concrete steps sending fresh adrenaline through his veins. The fourth-floor landing smelled of stale cooking oil and disinfectant, the scents of ordinary lives being lived behinddoors.

He paused before Apartment 407. Three quick raps. A pause. Two more. The rhythm they'd all memorized—a lifeline in a city where a knock could mean salvation or ruin.

The door opened just enough to reveal Sister Zhang's sharp eyes. She gave no greeting, simply stepped aside as Jun slipped through the narrow gap. Inside, the. air was thick with the mingled scents of perspiration, cheap detergent, and something else—that electric charge Jun had come to recognize as the presence of the Spirit.

They had no cross on the wall, no sign out front. Their Bibles were worn, passed hand to hand, often hidden beneath floorboards. Yet within those walls, the Spirit was as present as in any cathedral.

Outside, the Shanghai skyline glittered with surveillance cameras and facial recognition scanners. But inside that dim apartment, for ninety precious minutes, a dozen souls clung to a truth more powerful than the mightiest government.

They all knew the stakes. Just last month, an entire house church in Chongqing had vanished into the system—no trials, no announcements, just empty apartments and unanswered calls. The official WeChat accounts of those arrested had simply stopped updating, their last posts still cheerfully praising Party initiatives.

Jun's little group didn't know it yet, but heaven was preparing to make its presence unmistakably clear.

Jun Chao read aloud from Psalm 27: *"The Lord is my light and my salvation—whom shall I fear?"* His voice trembled slightly, but his eyes shone.

Then—the unmistakable sound of heavy boots on the

stairs followed by a loud knock rattled the door.

The group froze. The knock came again, louder this time.

Whispers rippled through the room. "Police." "We must hide."

Sister Zhang, whispered, "We pray."

They dropped to their knees. The knocking turned into pounding. A man's voice barked, "Open up!"

The knocks became louder. Jun Chao's hands shook as he clutched his Bible. His mind raced: would they be arrested? Beaten?

And then, in the midst of pounding fists and rising fear, something changed.

The atmosphere shifted—palpable, heavy with peace. A stillness fell over the room, silencing their panic. The pounding continued, but the door did not give way. It was no special door - and Lord knows the police were pounding hard enough and had enough practice at battering doors down - but it was though an unseen barrier made it stand firm.

Minutes dragged by. Finally, the pounding ceased. There was the sound of cursing. Footsteps retreated down the stairwell. Silence returned. The believers looked at one another, wide-eyed.

Outside, the night had gone perfectly still. Not even the usual hum of Shanghai traffic penetrated the silence. Jun Chao realized he was holding his breath, his entire body trembling.

He didn't understand. He couldn't explain. Whatever had just happened—whatever had made a door stand firm and hardened police officers leave an unarmed gathering—one truth became undeniable in that moment:

They were not, and had never been, alone.

A week later, at their next gathering in a different home, Sister Zhang brought an unexpected guest with her. A collective gasp rippled through the room as believers recognized the broad-shouldered man in civilian clothes—one they had been warned to fear, a persecutor of believers, now standing hunched and hesitant in the doorway.

Jun Chao's blood ran cold. *Was this a trap?*

But the officer's eyes told a different story.

Gone was the arrogant sneer. In its place—a raw, haunted vulnerability.

Sister Zhang placed a gentle hand on the policeman's arm. "This man came to my door last night," she announced, her voice steady with supernatural calm. "Not to arrest me—but to ask about Jesus."

Office Wei's testimony unfolded like something from the Book of Acts:

China Story A— The Unbeliever's Side

Officer Liu Wei had never once considered himself a superstitious man. He trusted in the Party, in the sharpness of his own mind, and in the authority of the uniform he wore. He had been taught since childhood that religion was an opiate for the weak, a superstition that shackled peasants to imaginary hopes. At the academy, instructors mocked Christians as dupes of Western propaganda. "Tools of foreign powers," they said. "Enemies of harmony."

Liu had believed them. Why shouldn't he? The Party had clothed him, trained him, elevated him from a rural nobody into an officer of the Public Security Bureau. He had authority, respect, a decent apartment in the city, even prospects for promotion if he proved his loyalty. That meant rooting out illegal gatherings — especially those called *house churches*.

When the assignment came down one humid summer night, he didn't hesitate. "Intelligence indicates a group of twenty meeting on the west side," his commander said, sliding a file across the desk. "Your unit will raid the location tonight. Break them up. Bring leaders in for questioning. Confiscate contraband."

Liu skimmed the file. A grainy surveillance photo showed a plain apartment block, nondescript among dozens like it. The report noted that neighbors had seen "suspicious gatherings" after dark. He scoffed. Suspicious gatherings — as if hymn-singing old women posed a threat to the state. But he understood the Party's obsession: control tolerated no rivals, least of all faith.

By 9 p.m. he and three colleagues sat in a black van a block away, waiting for the order to move. Cigarette smoke curled through the cramped space. The men joked to pass the time. "Bet they'll be singing about their *Jesus* when we walk in," one sneered. "Maybe he'll save them, eh?" Laughter filled the van. Liu smirked but said nothing.

At 9:30, the radio crackled. "Move in."

They slipped from the van, boots crunching gravel, uniforms blending into the shadows. The street was nearly deserted, only a few bicycles chained along the walls. The air carried the faint scent of cooking oil and damp concrete. They approached the stairwell of Building 14.

"Fourth floor, apartment 4C," Liu read from the file. He felt the weight of his baton at his side, the badge gleaming faintly under the streetlight. Power was a familiar companion, and he carried it easily.

The stairwell was dim, the single bulb above flickering. They climbed quietly, hearing muffled sounds behind closed doors — televisions, a baby crying, pots clattering. On the third floor, they paused outside 3C.

From within came the faintest thread of song. Not loud, not boastful. Just soft voices, unaccompanied, blending in harmony. The words were indistinct, but the tone was unmistakably worship.

"Open up!" one of the officers barked, slamming a fist on the door. The singing ceased abruptly. Silence.

They waited five seconds. Ten. The officer raised his boot, ready to kick the door in.

And that was when it happened.

Liu would later struggle to describe it. For years he had scoffed at talk of the supernatural. But in that moment, every hair on his body stood on end. The atmosphere in the stairwell shifted, thickened, as though another presence had entered.

The door, which should have been flimsy plywood, seemed suddenly immovable. The officer kicked once, twice. Nothing. The wood should have splintered, the lock should have snapped — Liu had seen weaker doors fall under less force. Yet 4C stood firm, as if reinforced from the inside by steel.

"Harder!" the commander hissed. They struck again, with boots and shoulders. The frame shuddered but held.

And then Liu saw it.

At first he thought it was a trick of the flickering bulb. A shimmer, like heat rising off asphalt, only brighter. But as his eyes focused, the shimmer coalesced. A figure. Tall. Radiant. Standing not in the stairwell, but *through* the door, as though guarding those within.

It was no blur of imagination. The figure was clear,

defined, yet somehow too luminous to study in detail. White, shining, unmoving. Eyes fixed on him.

Liu's chest seized. He stumbled back a step, baton slipping from his grasp and clattering to the floor. The others cursed, too focused on the stubborn door to notice what he saw.

But Liu saw. And he knew with the sudden, crushing certainty of a man confronted by something far greater than himself: this was no hallucination. This was no trick of light.

The figure did not move, did not speak. It simply stood, resolute, unshaken by their assault.

"Why won't it break?" one officer snarled, sweat running down his face. He rammed the door again. Futile.

Liu's voice trembled. "We… we should leave."

The others spun toward him. "What are you talking about? We have orders!"

He shook his head, unable to explain. His mouth went dry, words caught in his throat. He could not tell them he saw an angel — the very thought was madness, a betrayal of everything he had believed. And yet denial was impossible. The vision seared itself into his eyes.

The others tried once more, a final coordinated slam. But Liu was too afraid. The door held. From within, silence reigned, as if those inside already knew they were protected.

Finally, the commander cursed and spat. "Forget it. We'll return another time. Let's go."

Reluctantly, the others gathered their gear and stomped back down the stairs.

Liu lingered a moment longer, staring at the shimmer. Slowly, almost imperceptibly, the figure's gaze shifted to him — not hostile, but piercing. His knees threatened to give way. He turned and stumbled after his colleagues, heart hammering.

In the van, the men fumed. "Faulty intel. Bad lock. Next time we'll bring proper tools." They laughed it off, mocking, already planning excuses for their report.

Liu said nothing. His hands trembled in his lap. He could still see the figure when he closed his eyes, radiant against the plywood.

That night, he did not sleep. Every time he drifted off, he saw the eyes again — not condemning, but unyielding. He poured himself a glass of rice wine, then another, trying to numb the memory. It would not fade.

For the first time in his adult life, Liu doubted. He doubted the Party's assurances that faith was weakness. He doubted his own certainty that the material world was all there was. He doubted whether he truly held power at all.

For he had faced something in that stairwell, and in its presence he had felt powerless indeed.

Liu Wei filed his report the next morning with careful detachment. "Raid unsuccessful. Door reinforced beyond expected strength. Recommend heavier equipment on next attempt." He left out the part about trembling hands. He left out the shimmer of light. He left out the eyes that had pierced him.

The commander skimmed the page, scowled, and waved him off. "We'll circle back when resources allow. Dismissed."

Liu then resolved to do his best to ensure the address was forgotten.

That should have been the end of it. Another failed raid, another footnote in a career. But for Liu, it was the beginning of an unraveling.

The first crack came in his sleep. Night after night he

woke gasping, heart pounding, the figure still standing in his mind's eye. It did not threaten him. It simply *was*. Towering, radiant, immovable. Always between him and the door. Always looking at him.

He told himself it was stress. Fatigue. The residue of adrenaline. He had been under pressure; the brain played tricks. But the rationalizations never held. He had faced stress before — riots, brawls, tense interrogations. He knew what adrenaline did to the senses. This was different. Too clear. Too steady.

The questions gnawed. in the stillness before dawn. He began to wonder if the figure had not just been guarding the Christians, but confronting him. And he felt undone.

During the day, he tried to distract himself. He threw himself into routine — paperwork, drills, patrols. But small things unsettled him. Passing a church building sanctioned by the state, he found himself staring too long at the cross.

Then, an elderly woman bumped into him with surprising force. He was not to know it then but it was Sister Zhang. Before he could react, he felt paper crinkle against his palm as her gnarled fingers closed his hand around something illicit.

"Keep walking," she'd whispered in a thick rural accent, already melting back into the crowd.

His normal instinct would have been anger— but now the tract brought him wonder. Late that night, in the privacy of his room, he unfolded the little tract and read about a God who loved the world so much that He gave His only Son.

He stared at that tract. It was crudely printed, full of words he had been taught to despise: *salvation, sin, Jesus.* But this time, he did not despise them. He knew they were the truth.

He got his coat on and went to the apartment which a week before he and has colleagues had been battering on and knocked.

Story B from China — Light In The Cell

Her name was Mei. She was not a pastor, not a public figure, not someone who sought attention. She was simply a believer — a seamstress in a provincial city, known among friends for her gentle spirit and her quiet courage. She gathered weekly with a dozen others in the back room of a tailor's shop, where bolts of fabric muffled their hymns and sewing machines disguised their prayers.

Faith had cost her already. Her brother mocked her, her employer warned her, and once she had been fined a month's wages when police discovered Christian pamphlets in her bag. Still, she came. "How can I not meet with my family in Christ?" she would say. "If we are silent, even the stones would cry out."

One winter evening, the gathering was betrayed. A neighbor, pressured by the authorities, reported suspicious activity. The raid was swift. Officers stormed in, shouting, shoving, overturning tables. Hymn sheets scattered across the floor like frightened birds.

Mei was among those arrested. She was shoved into a van, wrists bound, heart pounding but strangely calm. She had always known this day might come.

At the station, interrogators demanded names of leaders, details of gatherings, foreign connections. She refused. The blows came quickly — fists, boots, a chair leg across her back. Pain exploded through her body, yet even as she crumpled, she whispered the words of Jesus: *"Father, forgive them, for they do not know what they are doing."*

When they tired of her silence, they threw her into a cell. Concrete floor, iron bars, a stench of mildew and sweat. A single dim bulb buzzed above. The door clanged shut, leaving her in darkness.

She curled on the floor, bruised and shivering. Fear pressed close — fear of more beatings, fear of never seeing her family again, fear that her faith might one day crack under the weight of suffering. Tears came hot and fast. She buried her face in her hands.

And then she became aware of it.

At first, it was only a shift in the air. The oppressive weight seemed to lift, as if someone had opened a window though the bars remained sealed. The darkness softened, though the bulb gave no more light than before.

She looked up.

There, in the corner of the cell, stood a figure. Tall. Luminous. Not dazzling, but radiant with a quiet authority that filled the room. Its presence did not frighten her. It steadied her.

Her breath caught. She whispered, "Are you…?"

The figure raised a hand, and though its lips did not move, words filled her spirit: *"Do not be afraid. You are not alone."*

Peace surged through her body like warm oil poured over wounds. The pain in her ribs remained, the bruises still throbbed, but her spirit lifted as though she were being held. She wept again, but this time not from fear.

She did not know how long the figure stood there. Minutes? Hours? Time seemed suspended. She simply knew that Presence had entered the cell, and that she was not abandoned.

When exhaustion finally overtook her, she slept on the cold floor with surprising ease. And when she woke, the figure was gone. But the peace lingered.

The days that followed were hard. Interrogations continued. Threats multiplied. "Confess your crimes and we will release you," they said. "Sign here. Deny Jesus. Save yourself."

She refused. Each time she returned to her cell bloodied and bruised. Each time, she remembered the figure. And each time, she found strength she did not think she had.

Other prisoners noticed. "Why do you not despair?" one asked, watching her hum a hymn under her breath.

Mei smiled faintly. "Because I am not alone."

Some scoffed. Others listened with quiet curiosity.

Weeks turned to months. She grew thinner, weaker, but her faith deepened. One evening, as she sat in her cell reciting Scripture from memory, the figure appeared again.

This time, it stood nearer, close enough that the light of its presence bathed her face. She felt warmth spread through her chest, steadying her heartbeat.

"The Lord is your strength," the voice resonated within her. *"Do not fear what man can do. For He who watches over you neither slumbers nor sleeps."*

She bowed her head, tears dripping onto the concrete. "Thank you," she whispered.

When the guard came hours later to drag her to another round of questioning, she walked with surprising steadiness. Her body bore bruises, but her spirit radiated something her captors could not crush.

One interrogator spat in frustration. "Why will you not break? We have broken stronger than you."

She looked into his eyes and, with quiet conviction,

said, "Because I have seen the One who stands with me."

The interrogator recoiled, unsettled. He struck her again, but his blows seemed weaker, less certain. She realized then that her witness was not only survival — it was a mirror held up to her persecutors, revealing their own powerlessness in the face of a greater Authority.

Mei was eventually released, months later, her body frail but her faith stronger than ever. She returned to her church, which had scattered and regathered in new locations. When she told them what she had seen, some wept openly, others nodded with knowing recognition.

For her, the angel was not spectacle. It was not proof to parade. It was simply mercy — God's way of saying, *You are not abandoned.* And though years passed, and persecution ebbed and surged again, that memory remained her anchor.

Whenever fear threatened, whenever interrogations loomed, she recalled the luminous figure in the corner of her cell, the hand raised in reassurance, the words spoken into her spirit: *Do not be afraid. You are not alone.*

And she was not.

Freedom felt strange after the months of confinement. Mei stepped through the gates of the detention center thin as a reed, her wrists scarred from restraints, her back still tender from beatings. The sun seemed too bright, the sounds of the street too loud. Yet beneath the fragility of her body was a steel she had not carried before.

Her friends from the tailor's shop wept when they saw her. They embraced her gently, mindful of her bruises, and listened as she whispered the story of the figure who had stood in her cell.

Some gasped. Others nodded, eyes brimming with

tears. One elderly sister said, "Yes, my child. Many have seen. You are not the first, and you will not be the last. When the furnace grows hot, Heaven walks with us."

From that day, Mei's testimony spread quietly among the underground believers. They did not announce it in loud gatherings; such stories were too sacred, too risky. But in whispered conversations, in late-night prayer meetings, her words became fuel for courage.

A young man facing his first interrogation remembered her story and found strength to endure. A mother fearing for her children whispered it to herself as she walked into another raid. "We are not alone," they told one another. "Even in the cell, He sends His messengers."

Mei herself returned to her sewing, mending clothes by day and meeting with the church by night. But she was no longer merely a participant. She became, without intending it, a pillar. People sought her counsel, drawn by the quiet authority that suffering had pressed into her.

When new believers asked if God truly protected His people, she would not promise them safety. She knew too well that some were beaten to death, some languished for years in labor camps. Instead, she promised presence. "I cannot tell you you will not suffer," she would say, "but I can tell you this: when you suffer for His name, you will never suffer alone."

And then she would tell her story again. Always humbly, always carefully, never embellishing, never sensationalizing. Just the simple memory of a figure who stood with her in the darkest nights, and the words that steadied her: *Do not be afraid. You are not alone.*

Years passed. Crackdowns intensified, then softened, then intensified again. Each wave brought new arrests, new martyrs, new stories. Mei grew older, her hair streaked with silver, her hands gnarled from years of sewing. But whenever persecution returned, believers remembered her testimony.

Sometimes young pastors would invite her to speak to small groups. She would sit in a dimly lit room, a single candle flickering, and recount her experience. Faces leaned forward, hungry for hope. When she finished, there was always silence, heavy and holy, before the prayers began.

And always, she reminded them that she was not unique. "I have heard many such stories," she would say. "Brothers and sisters in other cities, in other prisons, have seen his angels too. I am just one voice among many."

* * *

What makes Mei's account remarkable is not only what she saw, but how it contrasts with what Liu Wei, the unbelieving officer, saw.

He had encountered a figure at the door — immovable, radiant, protective. He could not enter. He was stopped, undone, confronted by a Presence he could not explain. For him, the angel was a wall, a barrier, a rebuke.

For Mei, the figure was a companion, a comforter, a friend in the darkness. Where Liu saw eyes that pierced him with unanswerable authority, Mei saw eyes that soothed her with mercy. To one, the angel was judgment. To the other, the angel was solace.

Together, the stories form a dual testimony. Heaven does not limit itself to the faithful alone. Sometimes it reveals itself to the persecutor, to shake him awake.

Sometimes it reveals itself to the persecuted, to strengthen their endurance. In both, the message is the same: the church is not abandoned.

Mei lived long enough to hear of believers in other countries who told similar tales — in Iran, in North Korea, in Eritrea. In Russia, Through whispered networks she learned that her story was part of something much larger, a tapestry of testimony woven by the persecuted worldwide.

Again and again the pattern emerged: when earthly power tried hardest to crush the church, heaven showed itself most vividly.

In her later years, when her eyesight dimmed and her steps slowed, Mei often sat by her window sewing quietly. Children from the neighborhood would stop in, curious about the gentle old woman. She would smile and tell them simple truths: "God is near. He hears. He sees."

To close friends she sometimes confessed, "I still see Him in my dreams. The figure in the cell. I think He is reminding me that one day, when I leave this body, I will not walk into darkness. I will walk into light."

And when she finally passed, believers gathered in secret to honor her. They sang the hymns she had once whispered in prison. They read the Scriptures that had steadied her. And they remembered the story of the figure who stood in her cell, guarding her spirit when her body could not be guarded.

Her life, like Liu Wei's reluctant confession, became one more stone in the altar of witness. One through the eyes of unbelief, one through the eyes of faith. Both declaring the same truth: heaven stands with the church, even when the world rages against it.

Reflection - Divine Bodyguards

We modern Christians have domesticated angels—reducing them to greeting card cherubs or supernatural butlers sent to find our car keys. But Scripture reveals a far more powerful reality: angels are God's special forces, operating where earthly and spiritual realms collide (2 Kings 6:17).

Officer Liu's story confronts us with uncomfortable questions:

1. The Visibility Paradox

Why do angels more often appear to persecutors than believers? Consider:

- *Pharaoh's household* saw Israel's divine protection (Exodus 8:19)
- *Babylon's soldiers* fell blinded before Daniel's angels (Daniel 10:7)
- *Saul's entourage* heard the heavenly voice but saw no man (Acts 9:7)

This pattern suggests a divine strategy—God allows enemies to glimpse His armory precisely when they threaten His people. Like celestial warning shots across the bow.

2. The Cost of Coverage

Angelic protection isn't generic—it's drawn to specific kingdom assignments:

- *Preaching* despite government bans (Acts

5:19-20)
- *Praying* when it could mean prison (Acts 12:6-11)
- *Persisting* in discipleship amid surveillance
- Partnering the preaching of the gospel (Signs and Wonders *follow)*

Notice: The early church didn't pray for angelic rescue until *after* they'd stepped into gospel danger (Acts 4:29-31).

3. The Officer Liu Effect

Every angelic appearance to unbelievers serves dual purposes:

- *Protection* for believers
- *Evangelism* to persecutors

Today in China:

- Over 60% of underground church planters report former officials now assisting their work

The Challenge for Western Christians

While our Chinese brothers and sisters risk everything, we debate whether spiritual warfare is metaphorical. Their reality checks our complacency:

- When was the last time we undertook gospel work *requiring* supernatural protection?
- Do our ministries threaten hell enough to warrant angelic reinforcement?

- Would any persecutors testify they've seen God's glory around us?

Jun Chao's parting words to me still haunt: *"Maybe American Christians don't see angels because they're never in danger for Jesus."*

The promise remains—but so does the question: Are we positioned where the promise activates? *"The angel of the Lord encamps around those who fear him"* isn't just comfort—it's a commissioning.

Next time you read about Chinese house churches growing despite persecution, remember—their 'secret weapon' isn't secrecy. It's the invisible army surrounding ordinary believers who dare to proclaim an extraordinary Christ.

Two Angel Stories: One Truth

Placed side by side, Liu Wei's and Mei's stories form a kind of living parable. They are not identical, but mirror images that illuminate each other.

Office Liu, the unbelieving officer, saw an angel as barrier. A figure of judgment, standing immovable against his authority, refusing him entry into a place he thought he controlled. He left shaken, his worldview fractured, forced to admit that he had met something greater than the state he served. The angel exposed his limits.

Mei, the believing seamstress, saw an angel as companion. A figure of mercy, filling her cell with light, whispering peace into bruises and fear. She left not broken but strengthened, her testimony fueling courage in others who would walk the same path. The angel revealed God's nearness.

Judgment and mercy. Warning and comfort. Authority and tenderness. To the persecutor and the persecuted, the same heavenly reality appeared, but its meaning was tailored to the heart that received it.

This dual witness is part of the brilliance of God's economy. He does not reveal Himself only to the already faithful, as if His concern were limited to insiders. Nor does He comfort believers alone, as if the persecutor were beyond reach. Instead, He extends revelation in both directions — unsettling the oppressor, sustaining the oppressed. One testimony presses unbelief toward doubt; the other presses belief toward endurance. Together, they declare: *the church is not abandoned.*

I have heard dozens of such accounts over the years, not only in China but across the persecuted world. Patterns emerge. The persecuted church, stripped of safety nets, often sees what the comfortable seldom do. Those who risk everything for Christ live with a raw edge of dependence — and into that desperation, heaven sometimes steps visibly in.

When I was working behind the Iron Curtain, I often felt the same pressing nearness. Sitting in a car at a border checkpoint, guards combing through luggage, sweat dripping down my back, I would whisper frantic prayers. And more than once, I felt a strange calm fall over me — a peace that bore no relation to the situation. I watched as guards suddenly waved me through, distracted, or ignored compartments they should have searched. I knew something beyond me was at work.

So when I sit with brothers and sisters from China, when they tell me of doors that will not break, of luminous figures in prison cells, of Presence that whispers peace into their suffering, I do not dismiss them. Their stories fit into a pattern too wide, too consistent, too weighty to ignore.

Scripture prepares us for this. Angels are not decorative extras in the biblical story; they are messengers, guardians, executors of God's will. They close lions' mouths. They strike doors open in Philippian jails. They surround Elisha's mountain when enemies encircle him. Their role is not to entertain, but to embody God's faithfulness in flesh-and-blood moments of terror.

And here is what stands out most: these testimonies do not create triumphalism. They do not make persecution easy or turn suffering into spectacle. Believers still weep, still bleed, still bury their martyrs. Mei still bore scars on her back until her final day.

But within the suffering, they bore witness to a Presence that refused to leave them. That is the true miracle. Not the absence of pain, but the refusal of abandonment. Not immunity from fire, but companionship in the flames.

This is the theology of angels in persecution: they are not primarily entertainers of faith, nor collectors of stories for Western audiences to marvel at. They are reminders, for persecutor and persecuted alike, that the God of heaven sees, acts, and stands with His people.

When I remember Liu Wei and Mei together, I see the two sides of testimony. One man hardened by propaganda, undone in a stairwell by a figure he could not explain. One woman softened by suffering, steadied in a cell by a figure she recognized as mercy. One encounter sowed doubt where certainty had once reigned. The other sowed courage where despair had nearly triumphed.

Neither story leaves us comfortable. Both confront us. If even the persecutor can glimpse heaven's guardians, then no one is outside the reach of revelation. If even the bruised believer can sing in a cell, then suffering does not have the final word.

And so their stories, like many I have heard from the persecuted church worldwide, join the chorus of witnesses stretching back through centuries — Daniel in the lions' den, Peter led past sleeping guards by a radiant messenger, Paul and Silas singing at midnight. Their voices add to the testimony that when the world seeks to crush the church, heaven leans closer, not farther.

I cannot say why God shows Himself more vividly in some moments than in others. I cannot solve the mystery of why some are spared while others are not. But I can say this: the persecuted church testifies with a united voice that they are not alone. And sometimes, heaven confirms that testimony in ways so tangible, even the enemies of the gospel are forced to admit it.

Two witnesses. One message.

So what do we do with Liu Wei and Mei? We listen. We let their stories trouble our tidy categories. We resist the urge to explain them away too quickly. And we allow ourselves to ask whether the unseen is nearer than we imagine.

Perhaps their witness is not only for China, but for us. For the moments when fear closes in — not in prison cells or police raids, but in hospital rooms, in losses we did not choose, in grief that feels like captivity. Their testimonies whisper the same truth: *Do not be afraid. You are not alone.*

A Final Word

If you have read these stories, you will have seen a thread running through them: in battlefields and hospital rooms, in prisons and on bridges. God has never stopped reaching for people. Angels are only one way He whispers, "You are not alone. You are not forgotten."

But the greatest message He ever sent was not through angels, but through His Son, Jesus Christ. Jesus entered our world, took on our pain, died for our sins, and rose again so that nothing—not even death—could separate us from God's love.

The Bible says, "For God so loved the world that He gave His one and only Son, that whoever believes in Him shall not perish but have eternal life" (John 3:16). That promise includes you.

Maybe as you've read these pages, you've sensed that tug on your heart. Maybe you feel the same gentle voice that many in these stories heard: Come home. You are not forgotten.

You don't need perfect words. You don't need to clean yourself up first. God asks only for honesty, for a willing heart.

If you want to take that step of faith, you can pray something like this:

"Lord Jesus,

I believe You love me. I confess I have sinned, and I need Your forgiveness. Thank You for dying for me and rising again. I open my life to You. Be my Savior, my Lord, my friend. From this day on, I choose to follow You.

Amen."

If you prayed this prayer sincerely, then welcome—you belong to Him. Heaven rejoices over one who comes home. Find a Bible, connect with a church, and keep walking this journey. You will discover, as countless others have, that you are never alone.

* * *

If this book moved you, please consider leaving a brief review—it helps others find these stories.

* * *

The next book in the '*When Heaven Steps In*' series to be released **14th October 2025.**

ANGELS IN ACTION: *(Book 3)*
ISBN 978-1-918219-09-8
Joe Lighthall

* * *

1st book of the series (if you've not already seen it!)

ANGEL MIRACLES: *(Book 1)*
ISBN 978-1-918219-05-0
Joe Lighthall

* * *

OTHER BOOKS FROM THE AUTHOR

Over the decades, Pastor Joe has gathered far more accounts than can fit between these pages, and so future volumes of angel stories—Volume 4, and beyond—are planned. Alongside them, he is preparing a separate series focused on miracles: testimonies of healing, provision, and divine intervention that, while distinct from angel encounters, reveal the same hand of God at work.

There is also another set of stories that cannot be ignored: accounts often described in modern terms as UFO encounters. Many of these bear striking similarities to angel visitations recorded in both Scripture and tradition. However, because the subject carries a great deal of cultural baggage—ranging from science fiction to conspiracy theories—the author has chosen to place these stories in a separate series.

This is not because he treats them lightly, nor because he seeks to sensationalize them. Quite the opposite. His approach remains pastoral and cautious, recognizing that many sincere believers are uneasy with the topic. By separating these testimonies, he aims to provide a careful, grounded exploration—free from the "tin hat" extremes so often associated with the subject—while also engaging readers who might never pick up a book about angels, but who are searching for meaning in unexplained experiences.

In this way, the distinction allows each stream of stories to speak clearly: angel testimonies here, miracles in their own volumes, and unusual accounts reframed with discernment in another. His hope is that, whatever form these stories take, they will help more people see that God is not absent, and that even in the strangest of places, His presence still breaks through.

LIGHTS IN THE NIGHT:
Christian Testimonies of UFOs, Angels & The Mysterious, Volume 1 (coming mid Oct 2025)
ISBN 978-1-918219-07-4

THE CHARIOTS OF GOD
Christian Testimonies of UFOs, Angels & The Mysterious, Volume 2. (Coming mid Oct 2025)
ISBN 978-1-918219-08-1

More to be released…

Follow Pastor Joe on Amazon Author Central or his publisher's website to hear about all new releases.

Have you experienced the unexplained?

Submit your story for potential inclusion in one of Pastor Joe's future books:

He's seeking credible, firsthand accounts of:

- Angelic encounters
- Unexplained rescues or warnings
- Precognition
- Medical miracles (against doctors' predictions)
- Supernatural provision in impossible circumstances
- Anything else 'weird' (eg: time slips)

Selected stories will feature in a future book (with full credit to you or anonymity if preferred - but note your name may have to be changed to comply with the law and protect others' privacy).

✨ WHY SUBMIT?

- Preserve your experience in a bestselling book
- Bring hope to others facing similar struggles
- Selected contributors receive: two free copies of the book (one for you, one for a non Christian friend)

🔒 OUR PROMISE

✓ Every submission read by our team (no bots)
✓ Personal response within 30 days if selected
✓ Zero spam—we respect your privacy

Email info@cosmicjivepublishing.com
Put "PASTOR JOE" in the subject line

Printed in Dunstable, United Kingdom

74464418R00068